Fat Free & Delicious

Ellen —
to your Good Health!

Robert Rez
2/98

Fat Free & Delicious

By Robert Siegel
The Healthy Gourmet

Pacifica Press

Manufactured in the United States of America.

Library of Congress Cataloging-in-Publication Data

Siegel, Robert N.
    Fat free and delicious : 176 fat-free & ultra low-fat recipes / by Robert Siegel
    p.   cm.
    Includes bibliographical references and index.
    ISBN 0-935553-13-4
    1. Low-fat diet—Recipes.   I. Title.
RM237.7.S558   1996
641.5'638—dc20   96-21772
                                                                      CIP

Table of Contents

FOREWORD

By John McDougall, M.D.

The most difficult and important task facing most Americans is changing to a healthier diet. Robert Siegel, The Healthy Gourmet, will help you have a better life by eating healthy foods that are better tasting than you ever would expect. Not only do they taste delicious, but you can eat greater amounts of these gourmet meals and still lose excess weight and become healthier. Having positive experiences like this at the dinner table is the right way to learn. Unfortunately, most people learn from the negative experiences of their failing health.

Americans are suffering from an epidemic of diseases. One-third of our nation is obese. Half the people will die prematurely of a heart attack or stroke, and one in three will suffer life-threatening cancer. The most important reason for all these preventable illnesses is the fat-laden, high-cholesterol, high salt, routinely processed, rich American diet. A meal plan that once only kings, queens and aristocrats could afford is now consumed by almost every red-blooded American.

You don't have to be a doctor, dietician or scientist to figure out the cause of our most common health problems. Look around the world to observe the health and appearance of various populations. People living in parts of the world such as Asia, Africa and the Middle East are trim and avoid the diseases that are common to Americans. Their diet is based on grains and vegetables. However, when these people move to America, they quickly lose their immunity to obesity, heart disease, high blood pressure, diabetes and cancer – because they change their diet.

The scientific literature points the guilty finger straight at our rich diet. Be aware of this situation. Armed with this knowledge, you can prevent serious disease, and regain lost health and appearance for yourself and your family. But change is difficult.

I hear people say, "no one wants to eat that way," because they think the food tastes terrible. The truth is, we often don't like new foods initially because they are unfamiliar. But only a brief exposure to new foods is needed to start developing new tastes.

Granted, some healthy recipes are tastier than others. That is where the genius of Robert Siegel in *Fat Free and Delicious* comes to your rescue. This book contains delicious, easy to prepare recipes that are good for your palate and your health. They are very low-fat, contain no cholesterol, and are high in carbohydrates and dietary fiber.

I personally have had the pleasure of eating many meals prepared from Robert Siegel's recipes. The ingredients and spicing are familiar to most people, which makes them a hit from the first bite. The difficulty of preparation varies: some dishes are easy for people with few kitchen skills or interest in cooking, others will intrigue aspiring chefs.

I'm sure after a few days of eating healthier meals from *Fat Free and Delicious*, you will ask yourself, "Why doesn't everyone eat this way?" Fortunately, every day thousands of people across America are making the switch. The changes end up appreciated and permanent when people like Robert Siegel make eating healthy fun, easy and delicious.

ACKNOWLEDGMENTS

I wish to thank the many people who have made contributions at every step of this project, especially these important people:

Wendy Baily, Jackie Baritell, Jeanne Bell, Sel & Sy Berkowitz, Joe & Gail Bickett, Jackie Burnett, Martha Buzza, RD, T. Colin Campbell, PhD, Robert Charm, MD, Allyson Clark, Ronald Cridland, MD, Indigo Crone, Mary Davis, Jack Dixon, Wilbur & Marie Dixon, Pat Emery, Roseanne Fink, Alan Goldhamer, DC, Joanie Greggains, Lola Haran, Lee Hitchcox, DC, Bob Jeruchim, Jim Knutson, Billy Leonard, Dr. John & Mary McDougall, Linda McFarland, Elenora Manzolini, Diane Marra, Sarah Martel, Diane Meikle, Bob & Joyce Neighbors, Pat Nowlin, Jeanie O'Neil, Dean Ornish, MD, Shirley Potasz, Joan Price, Cindy Renshaw, Keria Ritz, John Robbins, Yvonne Ruminson, Julie Sedgwick, Denise Shuster, Mary Small, Lee Strong, Jean & Ray Van Blarcom, and the thousands of Healthy Gourmet cooking class students.

Additional special thanks to Adele Siegel and Harvey Siegel, without whose support this project would not have been possible.

And a special acknowledgment and thanks to Sherryl Dever, my business manager and friend, who has guided me in making my dream a reality.

INTRODUCTION

Easy... fast... delicious... hearty... savory – these words describe the recipes in this cookbook. They're also as fat-free and guilt-free as they are flavorful, because these recipes use ingredients that are absolutely health-supporting: no grease, no grief.

Frankly, we debated whether even to mention to you that these recipes are also all vegetarian. If you're like most Americans, you may recoil at the notion of vegetarian food. You imagine it to be tasteless, boring, awful, choice-less, unsatisfying. You picture tofu-stuffed cardboard, brown straw, tree bark with sprouts.

Wait: look at the recipes we've included here. Look at the variations of traditional food you love: Sloppy Joes, Chili, Spaghetti, Baked Beans, Macaroni and "Cheeze," even sumptuous Apple Pie! We experimented with substitutions to old recipes until we developed the tastiest, most satisfying way to preserve the flavors you love while eliminating ingredients hazardous to your health. And look at the international dishes we've created: Lasagna, Deep Dish Enchilada Pie, African Squash Stew, Mushroom Stroganoff and many more. We've taken the best of the world's cuisines, taken out the fat, left in the flavor, and made them easy to prepare.

By the way, don't bother telling your family you're serving them "healthy" meals – just tell them you've found some tasty, new recipes! They won't even notice the absence of meat and grease!

You don't have to eat this way every day. Try once or twice a week at first. The more you can fit meals like these into your menu, the healthier you will feel and the more energy you will have. Cut the fat, keep all the flavor. Feel better, not deprived! And you may find you're enjoying eating fat-free and delicious enough to eat this way 50%, 80%, maybe eventually 100% of the time!

ROBERT'S STORY

I wasn't always a healthy eater or a healthy cook. I always loved cooking, eating and entertaining – but I did it with foods that were stuffed with calories and oozing with fat. I overate, drank and smoked. I never exercised.

My family history should have warned me. Every male member of my family had quadruple bypass surgery.

I quit smoking for my 40th birthday. Unfortunately, I had to start taking heart medication at age 42. "You're a victim of heredity," my doctor told me. "You'll have to take medication for the rest of your life." It was in my genes and I could do nothing about it. End of message.

By my 50th birthday, I had been taking medication twice a day for eight years. I was unhealthy and overweight, with no energy. "There's got to be a better way!" I told myself.

I decided to look into alternatives. After moving to California, I celebrated my 50th birthday by becoming a lacto-ovo vegetarian, meaning I gave up meat but still consumed dairy and eggs. I was also cooking with plenty of oil. No wonder I didn't lose weight, and my cholesterol didn't come down!

Then I found doctors like John McDougall and Dean Ornish, who promoted low-fat eating lifestyle changes for health improvements. After reading McDougall's first book, my initial reaction was, "This is too radical!" He endorsed a starch-based, meatless, dairyless, oil-free diet, a far cry from the cheese-smothered, cream-sauced meals in my menus.

Still, the more I read McDougall and Ornish, the more sense they made. I decided to try their methods for 30 days. The results were incredible! I started to lose weight and bring my cholesterol down. Changing my diet and lifestyle increased my energy and got me off all medication.

My first cooking attempts, though, were far from fabulous. I had been a gourmet cook for 25 years, and couldn't be satisfied with food that tasted bland and blah. So I started converting recipes and creating my own. Before long, I had learned how to make eating healthy savory, festive and fun.

My first cooking class was held in my house with nine people. Since then, I have taught thousands how to cook fat-free, delicious meals. I'm not a doctor or a nutritionist. I read all the information available and know how this kind of eating puts me and thousands of other people in control of our own good health.

Good health is a result of healthful living, especially healthful eating. This is a lifestyle change to a mouth-watering variety of foods even tastier and more satisfying than the comfort foods we thought we needed. This isn't a diet – it's what you're having for dinner.

24 CARROT ADVICE

↪ Make a conscious choice to take control of your health and quality of life through making informed choices about food.

↪ Find the source of the information you get through the media. Realize that the media get their "facts" from sources that often have a vested interest in slanting the truth. Call talk shows, write to authors, ask for the source of the information presented. Be sure that information is based on impartial, valid research that is not backed by some third party or ax grinding agency. "Milk does a body good" is sponsored by the Dairy Council. The old "Basic Food Group" charts passed to us through the education system in this country were provided to the schools by the meat industry. Just remember, where there is money to be made, there is a position to be taken in favor of the profit potential. It is our job as informed consumers to find the "real truth" so we can make the best, most informed choices for ourselves and our families.

↪ Read, read, read the labels on any processed foods. Be sure you understand what those percentages and goofy numbers mean. Please read the segment of this book explaining the "secret code" in food labeling.

↪ Keep it simple – take changes a step at a time! It has taken you decades to learn the ways of cooking and eating that are part of your life now. Cut yourself some slack, and be patient with yourself as you make new, healthful changes. You will need some new information to get what you want for your own health, weight loss or lifestyle. Use the Helpful Hints section of this book to get prepared.

↪ Be a student of change. Rapidly changing technology impacts our lives daily. As better research techniques develop and equipment for study change, so does our knowledge base. Stay open to well documented, well founded information that comes our way about any health related issues. Be wary of fads and trends. When new, well-founded information comes your way, be ready to investigate and integrate it.

↪ Use the new Basic Food Groups chart to assist in creating the right combination of foods for your meals and days.

↪ Consult your physician, especially if you are under care for any medical condition.

↪ Add regular exercise to your life to keep you healthy. Cutting the fat won't do it alone.

↪ Eat to live. Sustain yourself without deprivation. Eat for your lifestyle. Take into account: frequency of exercise, goals and personal desires.

NOW, let's get cookin'...

AUTHOR'S NOTE

This is not a diet or diet plan. It is a collection of fabulous mouth-watering, thoroughly tested recipes that can help you make better food choices.

If you are one of hundreds of thousands of individuals in the U.S. suffering from an illness and under the care of a physician, you need to seek his or her advice and approval before using the information in this book. We suggest you bring your recipe book to your next appointment and discuss how you should use the recipes to meet your individual health needs.

If your plan is to lose weight by eating less fat, you need to determine the combination of recipes that best suits your weight loss goals. Realize that even though we've eliminated high-fat meat, dairy and oil, some of our recipes contain a higher fat content than others. We have provided a nutritional analysis with each recipe so that you can see the calories and fat content at a glance. The fat percentage of the recipes that use tofu have been calculated using "lite" tofu. Using regular tofu will increase the fat content. The nutritional analysis does not cover any optional ingredients. Realize that if you include an optional ingredient such as nuts (or nut butter or nut milk), seeds, or tahini, the dish will be richer and often more flavorful, but also higher in fat. For most rapid weight loss, eliminate the recipes here that include nuts, seeds, nut butters or tofu, and build your way of eating around the vast number of recipes remaining.

Be sure to use the *New Food Groups* chart to establish your own best food combinations. Our "24 Carrot Advice" will also be helpful in taking control of your health through making good informed choices.

Breakfast

1

BREAKFAST

Breakfast is the easiest meal to make healthier. First, skip the high-fat, high-cholesterol breakfast staples such as eggs, bacon and sausage – they only clog your arteries, make you gain weight, and slow you down when you should feel your peppiest. Second, replace high-fat milk products with one or more of the many delicious substitutes available. Experiment with soy milk, rice milk, banana milk or fruit juice until you find one or more you really enjoy. All are great on hot or cold cereal.

Breads, bagels, muffins, French toast, waffles and pancakes can be wholesome breakfasts when made without added fat (eggs, butter, oil). Using whole grain ingredients instead of highly processed white flour makes these breakfast treats even more nutritious.

Always keep plenty of ripe, fresh fruit on hand as a healthy start for a busy day. A colorful variety of fruits offers inviting eye appeal.

On cold mornings, try reheating leftover grains from last night's dinner, topped with fruit if you wish. Or be more adventurous and try leftover Lentil Stew, baked potato or Carrot Loaf as a hearty, tasty breakfast!

For special occasions or a leisurely weekend brunch, you might want to try a fancier breakfast, such as Burrito Ranchero or Crepes with Fruit. No need to tell your breakfast guests these are healthy – just let them enjoy the delicious flavors!

BANANA MILK

(makes 1½ cups)

Serve over hot or cold cereal.

1   large ripe banana, peeled & sliced
1   cup water
½   teaspoon vanilla extract (optional)

1. Blend all ingredients in a blender or food processor until smooth.

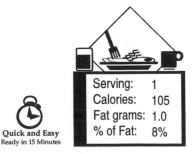

Quick and Easy
Ready in 15 Minutes

Serving:	1
Calories:	105
Fat grams:	1.0
% of Fat:	8%

BANANA RAISIN MUFFINS

(makes 12 muffins)

Dry

3⅓	cups oat flour
¼	tablespoon baking soda
2	teaspoons baking powder
2	teaspoons egg replacer (add to wet)
¼	tablespoon salt
¼	cup walnuts, chopped
¼	cup raisins

Wet

½	cup applesauce
1	cup honey
1½	teaspoons lemon juice
4	bananas (very ripe)*

1. Mix dry ingredients well.

2. Mix wet ingredients well with the egg replacer in blender.

3. In a large bowl, combine dry ingredients into wet ingredients and mix together well.

4. Spray muffin pans.

5. Fill pan to level and bake in oven at 325 degrees for 25 minutes. Check with toothpick. If still wet, bake another 5–10 minutes.

Bananas should have brown speckle spots to identify as ripe. Purchase bananas a couple of days before making muffins and let them ripen.

'Freezer Friendly'

Serving:	1
Calories:	265
Fat grams:	2.5
% of Fat:	8%

BASIC BISCUIT

(makes 12 biscuits)

Serve plain or with your favorite spread.

- 2   cups whole wheat pastry flour
- 1   teaspoon (rounded) baking powder
- ½   teaspoon baking soda
- 1   teaspoon Sucanat
- ½   teaspoon salt
- 1¼ cups soy milk (or rice milk)

1. Place dry ingredients in a bowl.

2. Add milk to center of ingredients. Carefully fold from center to the outside until all ingredients are combined. *Do not over stir!*

3. Drop by tablespoons onto a nonstick, lightly oiled cookie sheet.

4. Bake at 400 degrees for 10 minutes, until golden.

'Freezer Friendly'

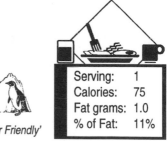

Serving:	1
Calories:	75
Fat grams:	1.0
% of Fat:	11%

BASIC BREAD DOUGH

(serves 8)

4   cups any combination of whole grain flours (whole
     wheat, spelt, oat or barley)
1   teaspoon salt
1   tablespoon Sucanat
2   tablespoons active yeast
1½   cups HOT water (130° – check with candy/
     microwave thermometer)
¼   cup WonderSlim or prune puree

1. Preheat oven to 375 degrees.

2. Place 1 cup of flour, salt, Sucanat and dry yeast in a large mixing bowl.

3. Heat water and WonderSlim or prune puree to 130 degrees and add to mixing bowl. Be sure to check temperature with a thermometer.

4. Add remaining flours (and whole grains), ½ cup at a time, stirring with a wooden spoon at first, then kneading with hands, or dough hooks on a mixer, or in a food processor using a dough blade.

5. When all ingredients are incorporated, knead dough until dough is smooth. It will not become as satiny as dough made with white flour. (With some combinations of flour and whole grains, hand kneading may be necessary because the dough will not follow the dough hooks.)

Note: You may have to add more water or more flour than the recipe states in order to achieve a workable dough.

6. Shape into 12 small dinner rolls, 8 large dinner rolls, 6 hamburger size buns, or 2 round loaves, and place on nonstick, lightly oiled cookie sheets.

7. Brush with soy milk or plain water and sprinkle with kosher salt. Let rise for *only* 15–20 minutes.

8. Bake dinner rolls for about 18 minutes; hamburger buns for about 20–25 minutes and loaves for about 30 minutes.

Helpful Hint

While all ingredients are being incorporated, you may add caraway seeds, herbs, lemon or orange zest, etc. for variety.

Option

1 or 2 cups of unbleached flour will make for a lighter, but less nutritious, loaf or rolls.

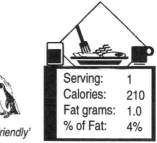

'Freezer Friendly'

Serving:	1
Calories:	210
Fat grams:	1.0
% of Fat:	4%

BREAKFAST MUFFINS

(makes 6 muffins)

Serve plain or with your favorite spread.

1	cup whole wheat pastry flour
1	cup oat flour
1	teaspoon (rounded) baking powder
½	teaspoon baking soda
1	tablespoon Sucanat
½	teaspoon salt
1	teaspoon cinnamon
1¼	cups soy milk (or rice milk)

1. Place dry ingredients in a bowl.
2. Add milk to center of ingredients. Carefully fold from center to the outside until all ingredients are combined. *Do not over stir!*
3. Spoon batter evenly into a nonstick, lightly oiled muffin pan.
4. Bake at 400 degrees for 10 minutes, until golden.

Options

Use half spelt flour and half oat flour for wheat free muffins.

For blueberry muffins, use 2–3 tablespoons Sucanat and add ½ teaspoon nutmeg. Use ½ to ¾ cup fresh or frozen blueberries.

Recipe can be doubled to make 12 muffins.

Serving:	1
Calories:	155
Fat grams:	1.5
% of Fat:	9%

BURRITO RANCHERO

(makes 1 quart filling; serves 8)

6-10 fat-free whole wheat tortillas
1   lb. firm "lite" tofu, crumbled
½   cup red onion, diced
1   small green bell pepper, diced
1   russet potato, diced
1½   teaspoons garlic, minced
1   cup salsa
     Pepper, to taste
     Salt, to taste
     Whisper of cayenne
     Turmeric to color

1. Steam potatoes for 10-15 minutes, until *al dente*.

2. Place potatoes in a sauté pan and sauté in half the salsa, adding garlic, salt and pepper.

3. Combine tofu, onion and peppers, and toss with potatoes. When they are just tender, continue cooking for 5–10 minutes (potatoes dictate the time).

4. Add the cayenne (*a pinch: be careful*) and turmeric. Turmeric will add color for an "egg" like color quickly, so add *slowly*, toss and decide if it's the right color. *Be careful, turmeric will add taste which you do not want!*

5. While filling is cooking, warm tortillas on both sides over a medium open flame until lightly brown. This helps make the tortillas pliable for easy rolling up. (You can warm in the microwave for 20 seconds for the same pliable effect.)

6. Place a couple of spoonfuls of filling in the center of the warmed tortilla. Bring the two sides together from the bottom and roll to the top.

Serving:	1
Calories:	140
Fat grams:	1.2
% of Fat:	8%

CREPES WITH FRUIT

(serves 6)

Batter

2   cups whole wheat pastry flour*
15 ounces sparkling water*
Pinch of salt

1. Put flour, salt, and just a little bit of the sparkling water into a food processor and blend until smooth as thick cream; no lumps.

2. Add remaining soda into the processor quickly and whiz. Do not over stir or mixture will become flat. Pour entire mixture into bowl. Keep whisk handy if stirring is necessary.

3. Pour small amount (no more than ½ cup) into hot crepe pan, whirling around to spread batter thinly. When bubbles appear, flip crepe over and cook for a short time; then slide out of pan onto plate. Serve hot or cold.

Flour and sparkling water should be the same temperature.

Filling

2   cups seasonal, ripe fruit or berries
1   cup apple juice
2   tablespoons arrowroot or kuzu, diluted in 2 tablespoons cold water
1   teaspoon vanilla

1. Bring fruit and juice to a boil in a medium sauce pan.

2. Add diluted arrowroot or kuzu and stir until thick; then add vanilla, stir.

3. Spoon approximately 3 ounces of fruit mixture into center of each crepe; fold crepe, then turn over.

Helpful Hint

Make extra crepes and refrigerate or freeze them for future meals.

Serving:	1
Calories:	180
Fat grams:	1.0
% of Fat:	5%

FRENCH TOAST

(serves 2)

Serve hot with maple syrup.

4   slices stale bread, sourdough or whole wheat
½   cup milk: rice, cashew, vanilla "lite" soy or almond
½   cup corn flakes, ground
⅛   teaspoon vanilla
½   teaspoon cinnamon
     Maple syrup

1. Mix milk and vanilla in a shallow bowl. Place ground corn flakes on a large plate.

2. Soak stale bread in milk batter.

3. Dip into ground corn flakes and lay on a nonstick griddle or nonstick fry pan over *low heat* until brown. Turn gently with a spatula; brown on the other side.

4. Sprinkle with cinnamon.

Option

Bake on nonstick cookie sheet, again turning and browning the other side.

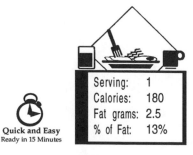

Quick and Easy
Ready in 15 Minutes

Serving:	1
Calories:	180
Fat grams:	2.5
% of Fat:	13%

FRUITED ROLL–UPS

(makes 12 rolls)

1   recipe Basic Bread Dough (See Index)
1   cup dried pineapple, small diced
1   cup dried organic apricots, small diced
1   cup raisins or currents, soaked in apple juice,
    drained
    Sucanat
    Cinnamon

1. Preheat oven to 375 degrees.
2. Break dough into 12–14 pieces.
3. Roll out into 8 to 9-inch diameter circles.
4. Spread dried fruit evenly on each bread circle.
5. Sprinkle Sucanat and cinnamon over fruit.
6. Starting at one side, roll tightly into a snake.
7. Form roll–up by rolling tightly into a spiral, tucking the end under.
8. Brush with water or orange juice and let rise for *only* 15–20 minutes.
9. Bake on a nonstick, lightly oiled cookie sheet for about 12–15 minutes.

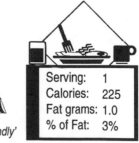

'Freezer Friendly'

Serving:	1
Calories:	225
Fat grams:	1.0
% of Fat:	3%

SCONES

(makes 12 scones)

Serve plain or with your favorite spread.

2	cups whole wheat pastry flour
1	teaspoon (rounded) baking powder
½	teaspoon baking soda
1	teaspoon Sucanat
½	teaspoon salt
1	teaspoon cinnamon
1¼	cups soy milk (or rice milk)
1	cup raisins or currents
½	cup dried fruit (pineapple, apricots etc.) finely minced
1	tablespoon orange or lemon zest

1. Place dry ingredients in a bowl.

2. Add soy or rice milk, raisins or currents and dried fruit to center of ingredients. Carefully fold from center to the outside until all ingredients are combined. *Do not over stir!*

3. Drop by tablespoons onto a nonstick, lightly oiled cookie sheet.

4. Bake at 400 degrees for 10 minutes, until golden.

'Freezer Friendly'

Serving:	1
Calories:	125
Fat grams:	1.0
% of Fat:	6%

Appetizers

2

BABA GHANOUJ
(Acorn Squash)

(makes 2 cups)

Serve as a dip or spread.

2	lb. acorn squash*
2	large lemons, juiced
2	large garlic cloves, minced
2	tablespoons tahini, toasted (optional)
½	teaspoon salt, to taste
	Freshly ground black pepper, generous
	parsley, finely chopped

1. Preheat oven to 400 degrees.

2. Bake squash for approximately 1½ hours.

3. Cut in half, cool and remove the seeds, discard; scoop out insides and place in bowl and drain off any liquid. (It may take a couple of times to get completely drained.)

4. Place drained squash with all remaining ingredients except parsley in a food processor and process.

5. Chill for two hours. Garnish with parsley.

* *A 2 lb. squash will only yield approximately 1 lb. after seeds are removed and liquid drained.*

Serving:	2 Tb
Calories:	18
Fat grams:	0
% of Fat:	3%

ADZUKI PÂTÉ

(makes 3 cups)

Serve pâté with crackers, toast fingers or crudite.

1   cup adzuki beans, dry
3   tablespoons tahini, toasted (optional)
2½ tablespoons tamari
1   tablespoon garlic, minced
½   teaspoon lemon juice
¼   teaspoon salt, to taste

1. Sort, rinse and soak adzuki beans overnight. Cook until soft, drain (reserve a little liquid to use, if needed).

2. Place all ingredients in a food processor and process until smooth. Use a little of the reserved liquid, only if needed.

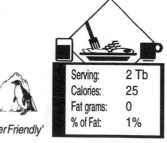

'Freezer Friendly'

Serving:	2 Tb
Calories:	25
Fat grams:	0
% of Fat:	1%

ARAM ROLLS

(makes 15 one inch pieces)

1   rounded cup Hummus, Spicy Red Safrito or Tangy Thai
     Dip (See Index)
2   cups red cabbage, finely shredded
1   cup carrot, shredded
1   cup sprouts (alfalfa or clover)
2   scallions, sliced length-wise (optional)
½   tomato, cut in ¼" slices
3   romaine lettuce leaves, ribbed & dry
1   package sprouted tortillas

1. Lay tortilla flat on clean board.

2. Spread Hummus, Spicy Red Safrito or Tangy Thai Dip evenly over all of the bread, especially on upper edge.

3. Lay vegetables in rows across the filling, making sure tomatoes are cushioned between other vegetables & lettuce.

4. Roll gently and firmly. *Don't worry – practice makes perfect!* Place seam side down.

5. Slice with serrated knife. *Don't press too hard when slicing!*

Serving:	1
Calories:	65
Fat grams:	1.5
% of Fat:	22%

BABA GHANOUJ
(Eggplant Dip)

(makes 3 cups)

Serve as a dip or spread.

2   medium eggplants
1   large lemon, juiced
3   large garlic cloves, minced
⅓   cup tahini, toasted (optional)
¼   cup scallions, finely sliced
½   cup parsley, finely chopped
1   teaspoon salt, optional and to taste
     Freshly ground black pepper, generous

1. Preheat oven to 400 degrees.

2. Cut off both ends of eggplants. Prick eggplants with fork in 6 to 8 places. Place on oven rack and bake slowly until completely collapsed, approximately 45 minutes. When completely soft, they're ready.

3. Cool and scoop out insides. Drain liquid.

4. Place eggplant and remaining ingredients in a food processor and blend.

5. Chill for two hours. Garnish with parsley.

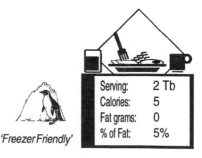

'Freezer Friendly'

Serving:	2 Tb
Calories:	5
Fat grams:	0
% of Fat:	5%

BEAN PÂTÉ

(makes 2 quarts)

Serve pâté on tostados, chapatis, in pita bread, bean enchiladas or as a dip.

3   cups dry pinto beans
1   tablespoon garlic, minced
1½ tablespoons onion, chopped
1   teaspoon cumin
¼   cup canned green chilies
1   lage tomato, chopped coarsely
2   teaspoons chili powder
1   tablespoon salt
1   cup salsa (mild or hot, to taste)
¼   cup bean water (from cooking), if necessary
    Pinch cayenne (optional)

1. Sort, wash and soak pinto beans overnight in three times the volume of water. Discard soaking water. Cover with three times the volume of fresh water.

2. Cook in plenty of water until tender (it could take 2 hours or more). Drain, reserving some bean water.

3. In a blender or food processor, combine well cooked beans and puree; add bean water, if necessary.

4. Add remaining ingredients and continue blending. Scrape the sides with a spatula and mix again.

5. Add more bean liquid, if necessary, for a smooth, thinner consistency.

Quick and Easy
Ready in 15 Minutes
With Pre-Cooked Beans

'Freezer Friendly'

Serving:	2 Tb
Calories:	25
Fat grams:	0
% of Fat:	0%

CARROT PÂTÉ

(makes 1½ cups)

Serve the pâté with crackers or toast, or as a dip with crudite.

- 3   cups sliced carrots
- ⅓   cup onion, diced
- 2   cloves garlic, slivered
- ½   teaspoon dill
- ½   cup water
- 1   tablespoon arrowroot dissolved in 2 tablespoons water
- 2   tablespoons white miso
- ¼   teaspoon sea salt (to taste)
- 2   tablespoons tahini, toasted (optional)

1. In a medium saucepan, sauté carrots, onions, garlic and dill in stock or water for 2–3 minutes.

2. Add water, cover and simmer until carrots are tender (about 20 minutes). You may have to add more water, so check occasionally.

3. Place carrot mixture in a food processor, add tahini (if used), miso and salt. Process to a smooth paste and return to saucepan.

4. Add dissolved arrowroot to the pureed carrots. Bring to a slow simmer, stirring constantly, and cook until the pâté detaches itself from the sides of the pan.

5. Remove from heat. Turn the pâté mixture into a serving dish, and let cool.

Serving:	2 Tb
Calories:	20
Fat grams:	0
% of Fat:	5%

HUMMUS

(makes 2 cups)

1   cup dry garbanzo beans (chickpeas)
⅓   cup water
¾   teaspoon salt
2   tablespoons garlic, minced
1½ teaspoons tahini, toasted (optional)
4½ tablespoons lemon juice
1   tablespoon fresh parsley, minced
    Dash paprika

1. Sort, wash and soak chickpeas overnight in three times the volume of water. Discard soaking water. Cover again in three times the volume of fresh water.

2. Cook until tender, approximately 2 hours. Drain.

3. Puree in a food processor with water until thick.

4. Mix in remaining ingredients.

5. Taste and adjust as needed. Garnish with parsley and paprika.

Quick and Easy
Ready in 15 Minutes
With Pre-Cooked Beans

'Freezer Friendly'

Serving:	2 Tb
Calories:	35
Fat grams:	1.0
% of Fat:	13%

LEMON CURRY RAITA

(makes 3½ cups)

Serve on baked samosas or as a dip.

1⅓ lbs. silken "lite" tofu, soft
¾   cup water
1½ tablespoons+ fresh ginger juice
1   tablespoon curry powder
2   tablespoons + 1 teaspoon lemon juice
¾   teaspoon salt
2   cloves garlic, minced
2   teaspoons honey

1. Blend all ingredients in a food processor.

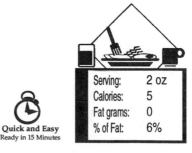

Quick and Easy
Ready in 15 Minutes

Serving:	2 oz
Calories:	5
Fat grams:	0
% of Fat:	6%

PIZZA WITH
ROASTED PEPPERS & VEGGIES

(serves 4)

2   red peppers
2   green peppers
4   large whole wheat pita bread
2   cups marinara, spaghetti or tomato sauce
4   tablespoons salsa
2½   cups onion, finely chopped
¼   lb. mushrooms, finely sliced
4   ounces soy mozzarella, thinly sliced

1. Wash, dry and quarter red and green peppers, removing stems and seeds. Arrange on broiler pan, peel side up. Broil 2 inches from heat for 10–15 minutes, watching carefully, until peppers are charred. Place peppers immediately in a paper bag to cool, closing bag tightly. Peel and cut peppers into small strips.

2. Using a serrated knife, cut pita bread in half. Bake in 350 degree oven for 3–5 minutes until edges are lightly crisp. Remove.

3. Mix salsa with marinara or tomato sauce. Brush sauce on each pita half; add sliced soy cheese, mushrooms, onions and roasted peppers.

4. Place in heated oven until soy cheese melts and pita becomes crisp.

Serving:	1
Calories:	295
Fat grams:	6.5
% of Fat:	18%

MOCK GUACAMOLE

(makes 3 cups)

1   lb. cauliflower
2½ tablespoons mellow white miso
1   cup frozen peas
4   tablespoons lemon juice
½   teaspoon grated lemon rind
¼   cup "lite" tofu, firm
¼   cup sliced scallions
2   large cloves garlic, diced
1   teaspoon ground cumin
½   teaspoon chili powder
⅛   teaspoon freshly ground white pepper

1. Separate the cauliflower into florets, using some of the stems.

2. Steam until crisp tender.

3. Steam the peas until tender, approximately 3–5 minutes.

4. Place all the ingredients into a food processor and blend until smooth.

Option

Add 1 tablespoon of your favorite salsa.

Serving:	2 Tb
Calories:	20
Fat grams:	0
% of Fat:	0%

ROASTED GARLIC

(serves 4)

Serve with hot soup and a crusty French or Italian bread.

    4   whole plump heads of garlic
    ¾   cup vegetable stock
         Salt & freshly ground black pepper, to taste

1. Preheat oven to 400 degrees.

2. With a sharp knife, cut off and discard the upper third of each garlic head, exposing the cloves. Leave the skin intact below the cut.

3. Set garlic heads, cut-side up, in a small baking dish or gratin dish just large enough to hold them.

4. Pour vegetable stock over the garlic and season lightly with salt and pepper.

5. Cover the dish tightly with a lid or with parchment paper under heavy-duty aluminum foil and bake for 1 hour, or until each clove is soft to the touch and the skin resembles lightly browned parchment.

6. To eat, scoop out the garlic puree from one of the cloves with the tip of a knife and spread on top of the bread.

Serving:	1
Calories:	40
Fat grams:	0
% of Fat:	4%

ROASTED RED PEPPER AIOLI

(makes 2 cups)

Serve as a dip, in Aram rolls or as a spread.

- ¾ lb. cooked garbanzo beans (chickpeas)
- ½ lb. roasted red pepper
- ¼ cup + 1 tablespoon lemon juice
- 2 tablespoons garlic
- 1½ teaspoons honey
- ¼ teaspoon white pepper
- 1½ teaspoons Dijon mustard
- 1 teaspoons salt

1. Rinse roasted red pepper well (if in a jar).

2. Blend all ingredients in a blender or food processor until smooth.

Quick and Easy
Ready in 15 Minutes
With Pre-Cooked Beans

'Freezer Friendly'

Serving:	2 Tb
Calories:	45
Fat grams:	1.0
% of Fat:	12%

SALSA FRESCA

(makes 3½ cups)

Serve at room temperature.

    1½ lbs. ripe Roma tomatoes
    1   red onion
    3   fresh jalapenos
    3   cloves garlic
    ⅓ cup cilantro, chopped
    ¼–½ cup lime juice
    ½ teaspoon tabasco
    ½ teaspoon cumin
       Sea salt, to taste

1. In a food processor, pulse tomatoes, onion, garlic and jalapenos.

2. Wash, dry and finely chop cilantro.

3. Combine all ingredients in a bowl. Refrigerate overnight.

Quick and Easy
Ready in 15 Minutes

Serving:	2 Tb
Calories:	10
Fat grams:	0
% of Fat:	0%

SPICY RED SAFRITO

(makes 2 cups)

Serve as a dip or filling for Aram Rolls.

1½ cups dry garbanzo beans (chickpeas)
6   tablespoons lemon juice
6   teaspoons garlic, minced
2   teaspoons salt, to taste
3–4 teaspoons mild chili powder
1   teaspoon cumin
2   teaspoons honey (optional)
½   teaspoon white pepper
2½ teaspoons Dijon mustard
     Bean water, as needed

1. Sort beans then soak overnight, in three times their volume of water. Drain and cover with fresh water (again, with three times their volume). Cook until beans are tender. Reserve some bean water.

2. In a food processor, blend all ingredients well to a creamy, smooth consistency. Add bean water if needed.

Quick and Easy
Ready in 15 Minutes
With Pre-Cooked Beans *'Freezer Friendly'*

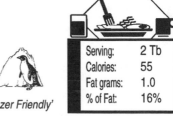

Serving:	2 Tb
Calories:	55
Fat grams:	1.0
% of Fat:	16%

STUFFED MUSHROOM CAPS

(serves 12)

24 fresh extra large sized, or 40 medium–large
    mushrooms
¼ cup water
1   large onion, finely chopped
5   cloves garlic, minced
1   teaspoon salt
2   cups packed, chopped fresh spinach, drained well
3   tablespoons tamari
1   cup whole wheat bread crumbs
    Freshly ground black pepper, to taste

1. Preheat oven to 350 degrees.

2. Clean mushrooms (with a mushroom brush), remove stems and set them aside.

3. Place mushroom caps, stem side up, on a nonstick baking sheet. Finely chop mushroom stems.

4. Sauté onion and garlic in water in a large nonstick frying pan. Cook, stirring for 2 minutes.

5. Add chopped mushroom stems and cook for 2 more minutes.

6. Add spinach and tamari. Cook for another 2 minutes or so, until spinach is wilted.

7. Stir in bread crumbs. Cook over low heat until all of the moisture is absorbed. Season with pepper.

8. Place a small amount of the spinach mixture in each mushroom cap. Repeat until all are filled.
Bake, uncovered at 375 degrees for 15–20 minutes.

Serving:	1
Calories:	30
Fat grams:	0
% of Fat:	0%

TANGY THAI DIP

(makes 2 cups)

Serve with vegetable sticks, pita wedges, or your favorite crackers or chips.

    2   tablespoons scallions, sliced
    2   tablespoons garlic, minced
    1   tablespoon fresh ginger, grated
    3   tablespoons + 1 teaspoon tamari
    3   tablespoons roasted almond butter (optional)
    2   tablespoons rice syrup
    3   cups cooked garbanzo beans (chickpeas)
    3   tablespoons rice vinegar
    ½–1 teaspoon tabasco sauce, to taste
    2   tablespoons sesame Gomasio (See Glossary)
         (optional)
    ½   teaspoon sea salt

1. Combine all ingredients except Gomasio and salt into a food processor or blender and blend for 4 minutes.

2. Add Gomasio (if used) and salt and blend for additional 30 seconds.

3. Adjust hot sauce to taste.

Quick and Easy
Ready in 15 Minutes
With Pre-Cooked Beans

'Freezer Friendly'

Serving:	2 Tb
Calories:	55
Fat grams:	1.0
% of Fat:	13%

Gravies, Dressings, Sauces & Seasonings

3

ALFREDO SAUCE

(makes 3 cups)

Serve over fettucini.

1¼ lbs. "lite" tofu, soft
½   cup soy milk or water
2½ tablespoons white miso
1½ teaspoons nutritional yeast
½   teaspoon onion powder
½   teaspoon salt
¼–½ teaspoon nutmeg
¼–½ teaspoon fresh black pepper
      Fresh parsley, minced for garnish

1. Blend all ingredients in a blender or food processor. Start with small quantities of nutmeg and black pepper. Garnish with minced fresh parsley.

Quick and Easy
Ready in 15 Minutes

Serving:	½ cup
Calories:	60
Fat grams:	2.0
% of Fat:	27%

B B Q SAUCE

(makes 2 quarts)

6¼ cups tomato sauce
1   cup tomato paste
1   cup honey
1   cup apple cider vinegar
½   teaspoon cayenne
½   tablespoon garlic powder
½   tablespoon onion powder
½   teaspoon white pepper
2   caps Liquid Smoke

1. Combine all ingredients except Liquid Smoke in a bowl.

2. Add Liquid Smoke until it reaches the perfect flavor for your taste.

Quick and Easy
Ready in 15 Minutes

'Freezer Friendly'

Serving:	¼ cup
Calories:	55
Fat grams:	0
% of Fat:	0%

BASIC ALL-PURPOSE MARINARA

(makes 6 quarts)

2   large onions, chopped
2   green bell peppers, chopped
14   cloves garlic, minced
2   lbs. mushrooms, sliced (optional)
5   28-ounce cans tomato sauce
1   28-ounce can tomato pieces
4   tablespoons sun-dried tomato bits
¼   bunch fresh parsley, finely chopped (or 1 tablespoon dry)
1   tablespoon thyme
1   tablespoon oregano
2   tablespoons basil
1   teaspoon celery seed

1. Grind all spices in a coffee mill, mortar and pestle or Japanese suribachi.

2. In a heavy gauge stainless or baked enamel lined cast iron pot, sauté onions, peppers, garlic and mushrooms in stock or water for 10 minutes until onions are translucent.

3. Add all other ingredients and simmer over low heat, covered for 1½ hours, stirring often (you can also bake in the oven, covered, for 1 hour). Be careful not to burn.

4. During last half hour, remove cover and continue simmering. The longer it cooks, the thicker and richer the sauce becomes.

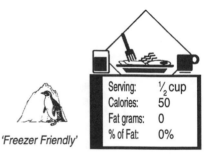

'Freezer Friendly'

Serving:	½ cup
Calories:	50
Fat grams:	0
% of Fat:	0%

BOLOGNESE SAUCE

(makes 1 quart)

1¾ cups canned crushed tomatoes in puree
1¾ cups canned tomato sauce
1   cup onion, diced
2   tablespoons garlic, minced
1½ teaspoons oregano
1   tablespoon basil
¼   teaspoon rosemary powder
1¼ teaspoons Italian seasoning mix
¼   teaspoon black pepper
3   tablespoons red wine (chianti)
¼   cup fresh parsley, minced
½   teaspoon garlic powder
    Pinch cayenne powder
    Apple juice, as needed
    Pinch salt

1. Sauté onions in apple juice, until translucent. Add garlic and stir while sautéing.

2. Add remaining ingredients and simmer on low heat for 15–20 minutes.

Option

Add tofu – 1½ cups frozen, thawed, squeeze dried, and crumbled. Add crumbled tofu and simmer for 5 more minutes.

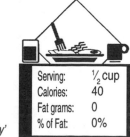

'Freezer Friendly'

Serving:	½ cup
Calories:	40
Fat grams:	0
% of Fat:	0%

BLACK BEAN AND GARLIC SAUCE

(makes 1½ cups; serves 6)

Serve over rice or baked potato

½   cup black beans, dry
2   cups water
16   cloves garlic
¼   cup balsamic vinegar
1   cup dry sherry
1½ tablespoons tamari

1. Sort and soak beans overnight in three times their volume of water.

2. Drain beans, discarding soaking water, and cover again with three times the volume of fresh water. Cook beans until tender. Drain, reserving all the bean water.

3. Place the cooked beans, 1/3 cup of the bean water, garlic, balsamic vinegar and sherry in a pot.

4. Cover and simmer for 40 minutes. Add more bean water, if necessary.

Option

You may want to blend some of the beans and liquid in a blender and return it to the pot.

Serving:	½ cup
Calories:	80
Fat grams:	0
% of Fat:	2%

CHICKEN–STYLE SEASONING

(makes 1½ cups)

1¼ cups nutritional yeast
1   tablespoon ground celery seed
1   tablespoon garlic granules
1   tablespoon sweet pepper flakes
1   tablespoon onion powder
1   tablespoon thyme
1   tablespoon parsley
½   teaspoon turmeric

1. Combine all ingredients in coffee or nut mill and grind until fine.

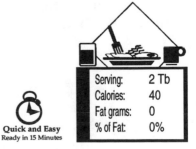

Quick and Easy
Ready in 15 Minutes

Serving:	2 Tb
Calories:	40
Fat grams:	0
% of Fat:	0%

COUNTRY STYLE GRAVY

(makes 1 quart)

Serve hot over loaves, rice or baked potato.

1½ quarts vegetable stock (preferred) or water
¾   cup whole wheat flour, pan roasted
3   tablespoons onion powder
1   teaspoon garlic powder
¼   cup tamari
¼   cup red miso
¼   cup nutritional yeast
2   teaspoons sage
2   tablespoons arrowroot
½   teaspoon thyme
     Salt & fresh black pepper, to taste

1. Reserve ¼ cup of cold stock or water to dissolve arrowroot. Heat the balance of the stock or water. After water has come to a boil, dissolve miso in a cup or two of hot water.

2. Roast flour in another large pot, stirring often: the darker brown the flour becomes, the richer and deeper in flavor the gravy will be. Be careful not to burn.

3. Add hot stock or water to pan of roasted flour, stirring to make a roux.

4. Add all remaining ingredients except arrowroot mixture; simmer for 20 minutes. Use a whisk to stir the gravy and remove any lumps.

5. While gravy is simmering, add arrowroot mixture to thicken.

Serving:	¼ cup
Calories:	35
Fat grams:	0
% of Fat:	0%

CRANBERRY SAUCE

(serves 8)

Good served hot or chilled.

1   lb. cranberries, rinsed
1   orange peel, grated (orange part only)
1   orange, juiced, plus water to make 1 cup
¼   cup honey (optional)
¼   cup maple syrup (optional)

1. Combine all ingredients in a saucepan and heat until cranberries pop.
2. Mixture will be slightly thick. Skim off any froth.

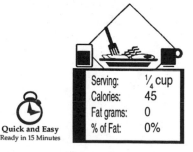

Quick and Easy
Ready in 15 Minutes

Serving:	¼ cup
Calories:	45
Fat grams:	0
% of Fat:	0%

CREAMY TOFU PESTO SAUCE WITH FUSILLI

(makes 5 quarts; serves 8)

Pesto

> 1¼ lbs. "lite" tofu, soft
> 2 cups water
> ¾ cups white miso
> ½ cup + 1 tablespoon walnuts
> 1¾ ounce garlic, minced
> 1½ cups fresh parsley, stemmed and lightly packed
> 1 tablespoon lemon juice
> ¾ teaspoon black pepper
> 1 teaspoon salt
> 4 cups (2 bunches) fresh basil, finely packed

Pasta

> 1 lb. fusilli
> 1 cup roasted red pepper (or diced fresh red pepper)
> 1 cup fresh parsley, minced
> 1 cup red onion, diced

1. Place garlic, walnuts, parsley, lemon, and miso in food processor and blend until smooth.

2. Add the rest of the sauce ingredients and continue processing until smooth.

3. Cook pasta in 1 gallon of water, until *al dente*.

4. Drain pasta and toss with the sauce, red pepper, parsley and onion.

Serving:	1
Calories:	360
Fat grams:	8.0
% of Fat:	20%

CURRY SAUCE

(makes 2½ cups)

Serve over fettuccine, rice, broccoli, cauliflower or asparagus.

    1   cup cooked brown rice (short or long grain)
    2   cups water
    ¼   cup nutritional yeast
    ½   teaspoon salt
    1   teaspoon garlic powder
1–2 teaspoons curry, to taste

1. Blend cooked rice and water until smooth.
2. Add remaining ingredients and blend.
3. Heat in a saucepan, stirring constantly.

Quick and Easy
Ready in 15 Minutes
With Pre-Cooked Rice

Serving:	¼ cup
Calories:	30
Fat grams:	0
% of Fat:	0%

TANGY LIME DRESSING

(makes 1 cup)

½ cup fresh lime juice
5 tablespoons + 1 teaspoon pineapple juice from
   frozen concentrate
½ cup water
1 tablespoon tamari
2 teaspoons Dijon mustard
2 teaspoons arrowroot
   Dash fresh black pepper (optional)
⅛ teaspoon liquid hot pepper sauce (optional)

1. Combine all ingredients except arrowroot. Blend at high speed in food processor or blender.

2. Pour into sauce pan and add arrowroot to mixture. Do not heat before adding arrowroot. Cook over low heat, stirring constantly, until a sauce-like consistency is reached.

3. Refrigerate before serving.

'Freezer Friendly'

Serving:	2 Tb
Calories:	30
Fat grams:	0
% of Fat:	2%

ENCHILADA SAUCE

(makes 6¼ cups)

3   cups onions, diced
2½ tablespoons garlic, minced
1   quart + 1 cup tomato sauce
3   tablespoons + 2 teaspoons chili powder
2   tablespoons cumin
2   teaspoons onion powder
¾   teaspoon coriander
1¼ cups water
¾   teaspoon oregano
2   teaspoons white grain vinegar
1¼ teaspoons salt

1. Sauté onions until soft and translucent.
2. Add garlic and continue to sauté for 3 minutes.
3. Add remaining ingredients and simmer for 15 minutes.

'Freezer Friendly'

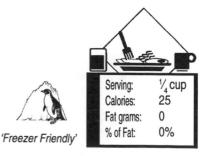

Serving:	¼ cup
Calories:	25
Fat grams:	0
% of Fat:	0%

GARBANZO GRAVY

(makes 3 cups)

¾   cup garbanzo flour
⅓   cup nutritional yeast
2   tablespoons onion powder (or dried minced onion)
¼   teaspoon garlic powder
3   tablespoons chicken-style powder
3   cups hot water
2   tablespoons A1 sauce
     Salt & freshly ground black pepper, to taste

1. Combine all ingredients except broth and A1 sauce in saucepan.

2. Toast over medium heat, stirring, about 2 minutes.

3. Dissolve chicken-style powder in 3 cups of hot water.

4. Gradually whisk broth and A1 sauce into flour mixture.

5. Cook, stirring vigorously with a whisk, until smooth and thickened. Serve immediately.

Quick and Easy
Ready in 15 Minutes

Serving:	¼ cup
Calories:	30
Fat grams:	0
% of Fat:	11%

GARLIC TOFU DRESSING

(makes 1 cup)

Serve over salad or baked potato, or use in potato salad.

¾	lb. "lite" tofu, soft
2	tablespoons Balsamic vinegar
1	tablespoon lemon juice
¼	teaspoon dry mustard
1	tablespoon tamari
	Pinch salt
1	clove garlic, minced
⅓	cup water

1. Place all ingredients except water in a blender or processor and puree until smooth.

2. Add water slowly until dressing is thick pouring consistency.

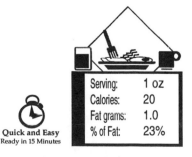

Quick and Easy
Ready in 15 Minutes

Serving:	1 oz
Calories:	20
Fat grams:	1.0
% of Fat:	23%

PINEAPPLE GINGER SAUCE

(Makes 1 cup)

Serve over vegetables, rice, Asian pasta salads, green salad, or use as vegetable dipping sauce or BBQ sauce when grilling.

1	teaspoon garlic, minced
1	teaspoon ginger, grated
1	cup pineapple juice, unsweetened
¼	cup tamari
¼	teaspoon guar gum

1. Sauté garlic and ginger in a little water in small saucepan.

2. After about 3 minutes, add juice and tamari.

3. Bring to boil. Then remove from heat and let cool. Refreigerate.

4. After the sauce is completely cool, stir in guar gum. Mix well with a whisk or in a blender.

5. Allow sauce to set for about an hour, until the sauce thickens.

6. Reheat or serve cold.

'Freezer Friendly'

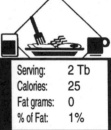

Serving:	2 Tb
Calories:	25
Fat grams:	0
% of Fat:	1%

GRAPEFRUIT VINAIGRETTE DRESSING

(makes 1½ cups)

Serve over salad or steamed vegetables.

1	cup unsweetened grapefruit juice
⅓	cup vinegar
4	tablespoons water
2	cloves garlic, crushed
½	teaspoon basil
¼	teaspoon thyme
1	teaspoon chopped fresh parsley
	Freshly ground pepper
¼	teaspoon guar gum

1. Place all ingredients in blender and blend at high speed for 15–20 seconds. Keep refrigerated.

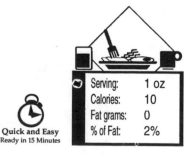

Quick and Easy
Ready in 15 Minutes

Serving:	1 oz
Calories:	10
Fat grams:	0
% of Fat:	2%

GREEN GODDESS DRESSING

(makes 2½ pints)

1 ½ lbs. "lite" tofu
2 ½ tablespoons chives, dried
1 ¼ cups fresh parsley, chopped
⅓ cups white vinegar
1 tablespoon onion powder
1 teaspoon freshly ground black pepper
2 teaspoons garlic, minced
1 tablespoon salt
1 ¼ cups water

1. Blend all ingredients until smooth.

Quick and Easy
Ready in 15 Minutes

Serving:	1 oz
Calories:	10
Fat grams:	<.5
% of Fat:	24%

SWEET AND SOUR SAUCE

(makes 2¼ cups)

Serve over rice or lentils, or use as a dip.

½   cup white wine vinegar
½   cup Sucanat
2-3 tablespoons tamari
4   tablespoons ketchup
1¾ cups pineapple juice (reserve ¼ cup to dissolve
    arrowroot)
2   tablespoons arrowroot

1. Mix together all ingredients except arrowroot and
¼ cup pineapple juice. Heat in a saucepan.

2. Dissolve arrowroot in ¼ cup pineapple juice and
add to hot sauce. Stir until thickened.

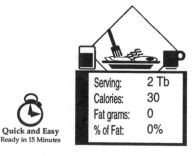

Quick and Easy
Ready in 15 Minutes

Serving:	2 Tb
Calories:	30
Fat grams:	0
% of Fat:	0%

KIWI DIJON DRESSING

(makes 2 cups)

Serve over green salad or fruit salad.

½   lb. whole kiwis, peeled
6   tablespoons apple juice concentrate
2½ tablespoons water
2½ tablespoons apple cider vinegar
1½ teaspoons Dijon mustard
      Salt, to taste

1. Place all ingredients in a blender or food processor.

2. Process until kiwis are pureed. If a thinner dressing is desired, add a little water.

Serving:	1 oz
Calories:	20
Fat grams:	0
% of Fat:	5%

LEMON DIJON DRESSING

(makes 1 cup)

Serve over salad, vegetables or baked potato.

4   tablespoons lemon juice
1   tablespoon tahini, toasted (optional)
½   cup stock or water
2   tablespoons scallions
1   teaspoon poppy seed
2   tablespoons barley miso
1   tablespoon Dijon mustard

1. Place lemon juice, tahini, if used, and stock or water in a blender; pulse to combine.

2. Add each of the other ingredients, one at a time, mixing well after each addition until dressing is complete.

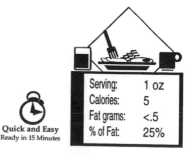

Quick and Easy
Ready in 15 Minutes

Serving:	1 oz
Calories:	5
Fat grams:	<.5
% of Fat:	25%

NUT "CHEEZE"

(makes 1 quart)

Makes sliced "cheeze" for burgers, sandwiches or snacks.

    1   cup cooked garbanzo beans (chickpeas)
    1   cup water
    ½   cup stewed tomatoes
    ⅓   cup cashews
    ⅓   cup lemon juice
    1   teaspoon ground celery seeds
    1¼   cup onion, chopped
    1   clove garlic
    ¼   teaspoon sage
    1   teaspoon salt
    ⅓   cup roasted red peppers, diced
    ¾   cup fine cornmeal

1. Blend all ingredients except cornmeal and roasted red pepper in a food processor until *very* smooth.

2. Stir in cornmeal and roasted red pepper.

3. Bake in a pyrex casserole dish, covered, at 300 degrees for 1 hour.

4. Let cool, uncovered, in the baking dish; then refrigerate overnight.

Serving:	1 oz
Calories:	30
Fat grams:	1.0
% of Fat:	25%

GINGER ALE GLAZE

(makes 2 cups)

Serve over stuffed butternut squash.

    12 ounces ginger ale
    ¼   cup honey
    1   tablespoon molasses, unsulphered
    1   teaspoon ginger, minced
    ½   cup lemon juice
        Pinch cayenne
    2   tablespoons arrowroot
    3   tablespoons apple juice

1. Place all ingredients except arrowroot and apple juice in a sauce pan.

2. Bring to a boil over medium-high heat.

3. Meanwhile, stir arrowroot and apple juice until smooth.

4. Add arrowroot and apple juice to sauce pan. Stir to combine.

5. Reduce heat and simmer, stirring, until mixture is thickened.

6. Glaze will keep for 1 month in the refrigerator.

Serving:	1 oz
Calories:	66
Fat grams:	0
% of Fat:	1%

KEBAB SAUCE

(makes 3 cups)

Use over grilled vegetable kebabs.

¼   cup rice syrup
¼   cup tamari
4   tablespoons mustard
4   tablespoons rice vinegar
2   cups water
3   tablespoons arrowroot

1. Heat all ingredients except arrowroot and ¼ cup water until simmering.

2. Dilute arrowroot in ¼ cup cold water and add to simmering liquid.

3. Stir until thick.

4. Pour some over kebabs. Reserve some for basting.

Helpful Hint

Prevent wooden skewers from burning on the grill by soaking them in water for at least half an hour before using.

Serving:	2 Tb
Calories:	15
Fat grams:	0
% of Fat:	7 %

PESTO SAUCE

(makes 1 cup)

1 large bunch fresh basil
1 tablespoon light or mellow barley miso
2 cloves garlic
4 tablespoons pasta water
4 tablespoons cooked garbanzos (chickpeas)

1. Pick off basil leaves. Wash and dry leaves (use a salad spinner, if you wish).

2. Blend all ingredients well. If too thick, dilute with a little pasta water.

3. Mix with your favorite pasta while cooked pasta is still hot. Serve hot or at room temperature.

Helpful Hints

Blanch basil leaves in boiling water for 15 seconds (until they turn bright green), then into ice water. This will prevent the pesto from turning dark when exposed to air.

Make lots of pesto sauce and freeze it in an ice cube tray (after frozen, pop out the cubes & put in zip lock bag) or in small containers for future use in sauces or over pasta.

Option

Use 3 tablespoons of pine nuts and/or walnuts instead of garbanzos for a richer dish.

Quick and Easy
Ready in 15 Minutes

'Freezer Friendly'

Serving:	1 oz
Calories:	30
Fat grams:	1.0
% of Fat:	15%

QUICK TANGY TOMATO SAUCE

(makes 1 quart)

Serve over rice, potato, pasta, vegetables or a burrito.

    1   28 ounce can crushed tomato
    1   cup onion, diced
    4   or more cloves garlic, minced
    1   tablespoon apple cider vinegar
    1   tablespoon lemon juice
        Pinch of salt, to taste

1. Sauté onion and garlic in stock or water until onions are translucent.

2. Add crushed tomato. Simmer 5 minutes.

3. Add apple cider vinegar and lemon juice. Simmer 5 more minutes.

'Freezer Friendly'

Serving:	½ cup
Calories:	30
Fat grams:	0
% of Fat:	7%

RANCH DRESSING

(makes 1½ pints)

Serve over salad or use as a dip.

2   lbs. "lite" tofu
4   teaspoons salt
1   teaspoon nutritional yeast
1   tablespoon celery, sliced
¾   cup onion, finely chopped
2   cloves garlic
½   teaspoon celery seeds
1   teaspoon dill
1   teaspoon dry mustard
¼   teaspoon paprika
1   tablespoon lemon juice
1½ tablespoons fresh parsley, chopped
2   tablespoons honey
¾   cup water
3   tablespoons distilled white vinegar
1   tablespoon chives

1. Blend all ingredients until smooth.

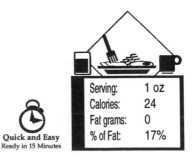

Quick and Easy
Ready in 15 Minutes

Serving:	1 oz
Calories:	24
Fat grams:	0
% of Fat:	17%

NO OIL RASPBERRY VINAIGRETTE

(makes 1+ cup)

Serve over salad or vegetables.

½ cup raspberry vinegar
⅔ cup water
2 teaspoons Dijon mustard
1⅛ teaspoons salt
½ teaspoon fresh black pepper
¼ teaspoon tarragon
¼ teaspoon basil
¼ teaspoon dill
2 teaspoons honey
¼ teaspoon guar gum
1 tablespoon shallot or
2 teaspoons garlic, minced

1. Blend all ingredients in a blender.
2. Let stand refrigerated at least one hour to thicken.

Serving:	1 oz
Calories:	10
Fat grams:	0
% of Fat:	5%

ROASTED GRAPENUTS

(makes 1 cup)

Use as a substitute for nuts and seeds.

    1   cup Grapenuts
    ¼   teaspoon garlic powder
    ½   teaspoon onion powder

1. Toast all ingredients together, careful not to burn.
2. Adjust garlic and onion powders according to taste.

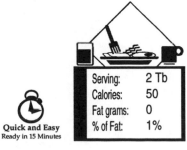

Quick and Easy
Ready in 15 Minutes

Serving:	2 Tb
Calories:	50
Fat grams:	0
% of Fat:	1%

SAVORY MUSHROOM GRAVY

(makes 1 quart)

Spoon over Holiday Loaf. Also delicious over baked potato, mashed potatoes or rice.

    4   tablespoons barley miso (traditional)
    1¾ cups stock or water
    1½ cups onion, french cut
    2   cups sliced mushrooms (approximately ½ lb.)
    2-3 teaspoons sage, to taste
    2   teaspoons thyme
    4   tablespoons arrowroot
    ¼   cup cold water
         Dash freshly ground black pepper

1. Spoon miso into 1 ¾ cup boiling liquid and stir to dissolve.

2. Grind sage and thyme with either a pestle and mortar or Japanese suribachi.

3. Add onions, mushrooms, sage and thyme. Cook for 15 minutes or more until onions are translucent, stirring occasionally.

4. Disolve arrowroot in ¼ cup water and add to mixture. Stir until thickened, about 5 minutes.

5. Add fresh pepper and more miso if a stronger gravy taste is desired.

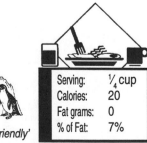

'Freezer Friendly'

Serving:	¼ cup
Calories:	20
Fat grams:	0
% of Fat:	7%

KETCHUP

(makes 1 quart)

1   cup tomato sauce
6   ounces tomato paste
1½ tablespoons cider vinegar
2   teaspoons tamari
¼   teaspoon onion powder
⅛   teaspoon oregano
⅛   teaspoon horseradish powder
2   teaspoons honey (optional)
    Pinch white pepper
    Pinch of salt

1. Mix all ingredients in a jar.
2. Store covered in refrigerator. Will keep for several weeks.

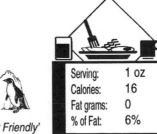

'Freezer Friendly'

Serving:	1 oz
Calories:	16
Fat grams:	0
% of Fat:	6%

SPICY ORANGE SAUCE

(makes 2½ cups)

Serve over steamed vegetables, brown rice, baked potatoes or pasta.

½ cup orange juice concentrate
1¼ cups water
1 cup onion, diced
3 cloves garlic, minced
1 tablespoon ginger, minced
1 teaspoon curry
2 tablespoons Dijon mustard
1 teaspoon salt
2 teaspoons honey
¼–½ teaspoon crushed red pepper, to taste
2 tablespoons arrowroot, dissolved in ¼ cup water

1. Sauté onions, garlic and ginger in a little water until water is gone.

2. Add all other ingredients except the arrowroot mixture and simmer for 2 minutes.

3. Add arrowroot mixture to thicken, and remove from heat.

Serving:	¼ cup
Calories:	40
Fat grams:	0
% of Fat:	4%

TARRAGON DRESSING

(makes 3 cups)

Serve over salad or steamed vegetables.

2   cups water
¾   cup rice vinegar
¼   cup honey
½   teaspoon black pepper
1   tablespoon tarragon (or more for stronger taste)
1   teaspoon dill
2   tablespoons garlic, minced
1–2 teaspoon salt
2   tablespoons lemon juice
½–¾ teaspoon guar gum

1. Blend all ingredients quickly, just enough to mix thoroughly.

2. Let stand refrigerated at least one hour to thicken.

Quick and Easy
Ready in 15 Minutes
(Let Stand 1 Hour)

Serving:	1 oz
Calories:	10
Fat grams:	0
% of Fat:	1%

TOUCH OF HERBS

(makes ½ + cup; serves 4)

1   tablespoon parsley, dried
1   tablespoon oregano, dried
1   tablespoon basil, dried
1   tablespoon thyme, dried
½   teaspoon black pepper
1   teaspoon rosemary, dried
1   teaspoon garlic granules

1. Mix ingredients together. Use in recipes that call for touch of herbs.

Quick and Easy
Ready in 15 Minutes

Serving:	1
Calories:	5
Fat grams:	0
% of Fat:	12%

TOFU MAYO

(makes 2 cups)

¾ lb. "lite" tofu, silken soft
2   tablespoons lemon juice
½ tablespoon honey
¾ teaspoon white pepper
½ tablespoon Dijon mustard
¼ teaspoon salt

1. Blend all ingredients in a blender or food processor until smooth.

2. Depending on the moisture content of the tofu and the smoothness of the mixture, you may want to add a little water when blending.

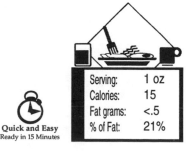

Quick and Easy
Ready in 15 Minutes

Serving:	1 oz
Calories:	15
Fat grams:	<.5
% of Fat:	21%

TOFU RICOTTA "CHEEZE"

1   lb. "lite" tofu, firm
½   tablespoon nutritional yeast
½   teaspoon onion powder
2   teaspoons garlic, pureed
¾   teaspoon salt
¼   cup parsley, finely chopped
2   teaspoons basil

1. Mix all ingredients with tofu until the consistency of ricotta – smooth and creamy.

Quick and Easy
Ready in 15 Minutes

Serving:	1 oz
Calories:	15
Fat grams:	<.5
% of Fat:	23%

TOFU SOUR CREAM

(makes 3 cups)

Serve over baked potato or any way you would use sour cream.

1	lb. "lite" tofu, soft or firm
¾	cup water
2	tablespoons umoboshi plum paste
2	scallions, minced

1. Blend all ingredients except scallions in food processor, until smooth.
2. Add minced scallions and blend for 30 seconds.
3. Refrigerate. Let sit overnight before serving.

Serving:	1 oz
Calories:	10
Fat grams:	<.5
% of Fat:	25%

Salads

4

APRICOT TERIYAKI RICE

(makes 2 quarts)

1¾ cups short & long grain brown rice (uncooked)
2⅔ cups water
1   medium carrot, shredded
2   ribs celery, diced
1   bunch scallions, sliced
¾   cup roasted red peppers, diced
1   cup baby corn, cut
1   cup water chestnuts, sliced
½   lb. snow peas, for garnish
2   tablespoons black sesame seeds

Sauce   *(approximately 2 cups)*

⅔   cup tamari
¾   cup rice vinegar
½   cup honey
¼   cup apricot preserves (or dried apricots)
2   teaspoons garlic, minced
1   teaspoon garlic powder
1   teaspoon onion powder
1   teaspoon dry mustard
2   tablespoons fresh ginger
¼   teaspoon guar gum
1½ teaspoons five spice

1. Cook rice in water, covered, for 40 minutes until water is absorbed.

2. Mix all ingredients for sauce in a blender until ginger is pureed.

3. Toss all vegetables, rice and sauce together. Serve at room temperature.

Serving:	1 cup
Calories:	325
Fat grams:	3.0
% of Fat:	8%

ARTICHOKE SALAD

(serves 4)

2   cups artichoke hearts, quartered (packed in water)
4   Roma tomatoes, sliced
2   scallions, sliced
1   cup cooked red kidney beans
½   cup carrots, julienned and steamed *al dente*
     Tangy Pepper Vinaigrette Dressing (See below)

1. Place vegetables in a bowl.

2. Sprinkle with Tangy Pepper Vinaigrette and gently toss. Serve at room temperature.

TANGY PEPPER VINAIGRETTE

(makes 2½ cups)

8   tablespoons fresh squeezed lemon juice
2   teaspoons Dijon mustard
¼   cup roasted red peppers
8   ounce can peeled tomatoes, drained, reserve juice
½   cup water (use juice of tomatoes, if available)
¼   cup apple juice
     Dash freshly ground black pepper
1   tablespoon oregano
⅛   teaspoon cayenne pepper
1   teaspoon marjoram
2   teaspoons basil
2   cloves garlic
1½   teaspoons tamari

1. Blend all ingredients for 10–20 seconds.

Serving:	1
Calories:	120
Fat grams:	1.0
% of Fat:	4%

ASPARAGUS SALAD

(serves 4)

1   lb. asparagus
¼   cup red onion, finely diced
¼   cup water chestnuts, sliced
      Grapefruit Vinaigrette Dressing (See Index)
¼   fresh red pepper, julienne

1. Prepare asparagus by snapping off the tough ends. Steam 4–5 minutes.

2. Lay cooked asparagus on a plate (preferably oval). Lay onions and water chestnuts on top.

3. Sprinkle Grapefruit Vinaigrette over all. Garnish with red pepper julienne strips. Serve at room temperature.

Serving:	1
Calories:	35
Fat grams:	0
% of Fat:	0%

BEET SALAD

(serves 4)

3   medium beets, cooked, sliced in half moons
3   medium tart apples, quartered, unpeeled, sliced
¼   cup red onion, finely diced
1   bunch watercress, washed, spun dry
    French Dressing (See below)

1. Cut off beet greens (can steam with other vegetables, if used right away), leaving a couple of inches attached to beets. Rinse. Place in large pot of boiling water and cook for 40–50 minutes, depending on size.

2. Rinse in cold water and slip off skins.

3. Slice beets, cut in halves and place in a bowl. Let cool.

4. Gently toss beets, apples and red onion together.

5. Place watercress on individual plates. Place beet and apple mixture on top of watercress.

6. Drizzle French Dressing over salad. Serve chilled.

FRENCH DRESSING

(makes 1 cup)

½   cup water
3   tablespoons lemon juice
¼   teaspoon salt
¼   teaspoon Sucanat
⅛   teaspoon freshly ground black
     pepper
¼   teaspoon dry mustard
¼   teaspoon paprika
⅛   teaspoon guar gum

1. Blend all ingredients in a blender.

2. Place in cruet or covered jar and chill for 1 hour. Shake before serving.

Serving:	1
Calories:	80
Fat grams:	0
% of Fat:	0%

EGGLESS EGG SALAD

(makes 1 quart)

1¼ lbs. "lite" tofu, extra firm
3   tablespoons Dijon mustard
2   teaspoons salt
1½ teaspoons distilled vinegar
1½ teaspoons cider vinegar
2   tablespoons water
1½ teaspoons honey
      Pinch of cayenne
1½ teaspoons lemon juice
½   teaspoon turmeric
¼   cup red onion, diced
1½ cups celery, diced
¼   cup scallion, diced

1. Mix together Dijon mustard, cider vinegar, distilled vinegar, water, honey, cayenne, lemon juice and turmeric.

2. Crumble drained tofu in a food processor. *Do not* let tofu get mushy. Add above ingredients before tofu is broken down.

3. Add red onions, celery and scallions and blend gently by hand.

Serving:	½ cup
Calories:	45
Fat grams:	1.0
% of Fat:	25%

FRUITED COLE SLAW

(makes 2 quarts)

Vegetables

1	lb. cabbage, thinly sliced
½	lb. carrots, shredded
1	cup raisins

Dressing

1	cup Tofu Mayo (See Index)
3	tablespoons apple cider vinegar
2½	ounce apple juice concentrate
1	cup onion, chopped
1	tablespoon honey

1. Mix dressing in a blender.
2. Toss all ingredients together.

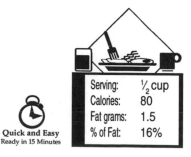

Quick and Easy
Ready in 15 Minutes

Serving:	½ cup
Calories:	80
Fat grams:	1.5
% of Fat:	16%

HOT GERMAN POTATO SALAD

(makes 2 quarts)

2½ lbs. red potatoes, unpeeled
1   cup celery, diced
1   cup red or green pepper, diced
1½ cups onion, diced
3   tablespoons whole wheat flour
¾   cup water
⅓   cup tahini, toasted (optional)
¾   teaspoon Liquid Smoke
2   tablespoons Sucanat
3   tablespoons cider vinegar
3   tablespoons tarragon vinegar
1   teaspoon salt
      Dash freshly ground black pepper

1. Boil red potatoes until done, but firm.

2. Sauté celery, pepper, and onion in stock or water until crisp tender.

3. Combine flour, water, tahini (if used) and Liquid Smoke and add to the sautéed vegetables. Stir well.

4. Combine Sucanat, cider vinegar, tarragon vinegar, salt and pepper, and add to sauté mixture. Stir well.

5. Dice hot boiled potatoes into large chunks and place in a large bowl. Add vegetable mixture and toss gently to coat the potatoes. Serve hot or cold.

Serving:	1 cup
Calories:	140
Fat grams:	0
% of Fat:	2%

MEXICAN POTATO SALAD

(serves 6)

2   lbs. red potatoes, cut in chunks
1   cup frozen corn kernels (thawed)
1   large tomato, chopped
1   bunch scallions, sliced
½ cup mild salsa
2½ tablespoons lime juice
1   tablespoon cilantro, chopped
2   tablespoons parsley, chopped
    Salt, to taste
    Freshly ground black pepper, to taste

1. Cook potatoes until done, but firm.

2. Combine all ingredients; toss gently, making sure to coat the potatoes. Serve at room temperature.

Serving:	½ cup
Calories:	115
Fat grams:	0
% of Fat:	0%

ORANGE & ONION SALAD

(serves 4)

1   head butter lettuce
2   large navel oranges, peeled, thinly sliced
½   medium red onion, thinly sliced
     Orange Mustard Dressing (See below)

1. Wash lettuce and spin dry. Separate the leaves.

2. Prepare oranges and onions.

3. Arrange lettuce leaves on a large plate. Arrange orange pieces on top of lettuce leaves. Arrange onions on top of orange pieces.

4. Sprinkle Orange Mustard Dressing over all. Serve at room temperature or chilled.

ORANGE MUSTARD DRESSING

(makes 2 cups)

5   ounces orange juice concentrate
1½   cups water
3   tablespoons apple cider vinegar
3   tablespoons Dijon mustard
4   tablespoons onion, chopped
⅛   teaspoon white pepper
1   teaspoon salt
½   teaspoon guar gum

1. Blend all ingredients in a blender or food processor until smooth.

Quick and Easy
Ready in 15 Minutes

Serving:	1
Calories:	55
Fat grams:	0
% of Fat:	3%

POTATO DIJONNAISE

(makes 1½ quarts)

6   cups red potatoes, cut in eighths
1½ cups Tofu Mayo (See Index)
¼   cup Dijon mustard
1   cup celery, sliced
¾   cup scallions, sliced
⅓   cup red onion, diced
1   teaspoon salt
1½ teaspoons white vinegar
1½ teaspoons honey
   Pinch white pepper

1. Make tofu mayonnaise.

2. Cut potatoes and boil until *al dente*. Drain and let cool.

3. Make sauce with mayo, Dijon, salt, vinegar, honey and pepper.

4. Combine cooled potatoes with vegetables and gently toss with sauce.

Serving:	1 cup
Calories:	185
Fat grams:	3.0
% of Fat:	15%

ROMAINE SALAD

(Serves 6)

1   head romaine lettuce
1   cup red cabbage, thinly sliced
1   cup celery, sliced
1   handful mung or sunflower sprouts
1   cup water-packed artichoke hearts, quartered and
    cut in halves (optional)
12–14 cherry tomatoes
    Raspberry Vinaigrette Dressing (See Index)

1. Wash lettuce and spin dry. Chop or hand tear into salad bowl.
2. Add remaining ingredients. Add enough salad dressing to cling, not soak.
3. Toss gently.

Option

Red cabbage can be cut in thicker slices then cut in half, your choice. Choose from a variety of oil-free dressings or simply sprinkle with Balsamic vinegar.

Quick and Easy
Ready in 15 Minutes

Serving:	1
Calories:	40
Fat grams:	0
% of Fat:	8%

SPINACH & SUN-DRIED TOMATO SALAD

(serves 8)

1½ lb. spinach, stems removed, washed and spun dried
1   large handful alfalfa sprouts
1   large handful mung bean sprouts
1   cup sun-dried tomato bits
¼   cup Roasted Grapenuts (See Index)
     Green Goddess Dressing (See Index)

1. Toss all ingredients except Roasted Grapenuts in a large salad bowl, with just enough dressing to cling. Sprinkle Roasted Grapenuts on top.

Serving:	1
Calories:	135
Fat grams:	2.0
% of Fat:	11%

SPINACH & CAULIFLOWER SALAD

(serves 6)

1½ lb. spinach, stems removed, washed and spun dried
2   cups raw cauliflower florets
½   cup red pepper, diced
½   cup yellow pepper, diced
1   cup mung bean sprouts
½   cup almonds, slivered (optional)
     Tarragon Dressing (See Index)

1. Toss all ingredients in a large salad bowl, with just enough dressing to cling.

Quick and Easy
Ready in 15 Minutes

Serving:	½ oz.
Calories:	65
Fat grams:	1.0
% of Fat:	8%

SPRING GARDEN VEGETABLE SALAD

(serves 6)

1   head romaine lettuce
1   head butter lettuce
6   Roma tomatoes, chopped
1   cup alfalfa or sunflower sprouts
1   cup broccoli florets, steamed
1   cup cauliflower florets, steamed
1   cup zucchini, cubed and sautéed
1   cup yellow squash, cubed and sautéed
1   cup snow peas, blanched and halved
1   cup fresh English peas, raw
    Ranch Dressing (See Index)

1. Wash lettuce and spin dry. Chop or hand tear into a large salad bowl.
2. Add tomatoes and sprouts.
3. Toss in cooked vegetables.
4. Add enough salad dressing to cling.

Serving:	1
Calories:	95
Fat grams:	2.0
% of Fat:	18%

SUMMER RICE SALAD

(serves 8)

Salad

4	cups long grain brown rice, cooked
½	cup onion, chopped
½	cup celery, finely diced
½	cup cucumber, finely diced (optional)
¼	cup green pepper, finely diced
¼	cup red pepper, finely diced
¼	cup fresh parsley, finely minced

Dressing

2	tablespoons red wine vinegar
½	teaspoon salt
⅓	cup water
	Pinch of freshly ground black pepper
½	teaspoon tarragon
⅛	teaspoon guar gum

1. Mix all dressing ingredients in a blender. Allow mixture to chill for 1 hour to thicken.

2. Combine and toss all salad ingredients and dressing in a bowl. Garnish with fresh minced parsley. Serve chilled.

Serving:	1
Calories:	120
Fat grams:	1.0
% of Fat:	7%

VEGETABLE TABOULI

(serves 6)

1   cup bulgur (medium cracked wheat)
8   ounce can water chestnuts, drained, chopped
½   cup scallions, minced
½   cup carrot, chopped
⅓   cup fresh mint, chopped
¼   teaspoon vegetable chicken-style broth powder,
    dissolved in ¼ cup water
¼   cup lemon juice
    Sea salt, to taste
2   medium ripe tomatoes
    Romaine leaves, washed and crisp
    Fresh mint sprigs

1. Rinse bulgur well in a strainer and drain.

2. Combine bulgur with 1 cup cold water and let stand in a bowl until soft to bite, approximately 1 hour. Drain any remaining liquid.

3. Mix bulgur with water chestnuts, onions, carrots, chopped mint, broth and lemon juice. Add salt to taste.

4. To serve, spoon into a wide shallow bowl. Slice tomatoes into thin wedges, enough to make 1–2 tablespoons.

5. Invert bowl onto platter and line wedged tomatoes around edge, leaning against salad. Sprinkle chopped tomatoes over mixture and garnish with fresh mint sprigs.

Serving:	1
Calories:	120
Fat grams:	1.0
% of Fat:	4%

TERIYAKI NOODLES
(serves 6)

Serve as an entrée or salad.

½ cup sesame seeds, toasted (optional)
½ lb. carrots (2 medium), julienne
¼ lb. roasted red pepper, diced
¾ lb. celery (6 ribs), diagonal sliced
¼ lb. scallions, diagonal sliced
¼ cup black sesame seeds, toasted
½ lb. baked tofu, triangles (optional)
1   lb. linguini noodles or spelt pasta

Teriyaki Sauce   *(makes 1½ – 2 cups)*

½ cup tamári
¾ cup rice vinegar
3½ tablespoons honey
1¾ teaspoons garlic, minced
¾ teaspoon garlic powder
1   teaspoon onion powder
¾ teaspoon dry mustard
3½ tablespoons ginger juice
¼ rounded teaspoon guar gum

1. Roast sesame seeds, if used, in 350 degree oven for 6–7 minutes. Shake or stir so they bake evenly.
2. Cut vegetables (into oriental shapes, if desired).
3. Mince garlic.
4. Finely mince ginger with a little water.
5. Blend all sauce ingredients for 30–60 seconds and let sit for 30 minutes to allow guar gum to thicken.
6. Cook pasta in 1 gallon water until *al dente*.
7. Toss pasta and vegetables in sauce. Let pasta marinate for ½ hour then toss again. Garnish with more black sesame seeds and slivered scallions, if desired.

Serving:	1
Calories:	345
Fat grams:	1.5
% of Fat:	4%

TOMATO MANGO SALAD

(serves 4)

2   ripe mangoes, peeled & cubed
4   ripe Roma tomatoes, cubed
12–14 fresh basil leaves, thinly sliced in strips
4   tablespoons Balsamic vinegar

1. Place tomato and mango cubes in a bowl.
2. Sprinkle basil slices over the cubes.
3. Drizzle vinegar over the salad and gently toss.

Helpful Hint

Purchase the mangoes a few days before to make sure they are ripe.

Option

Fresh mint leaves can be substituted for the basil for a different taste.

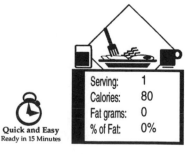

Quick and Easy
Ready in 15 Minutes

Serving:	1
Calories:	80
Fat grams:	0
% of Fat:	0%

TUSCAN BEAN SALAD

(serves 6)

2   cups cooked navy beans
1   lb. green beans, trimmed, cut in half and steamed
1   lb. small red potatoes, cut in half and steamed
4   scallions, thinly sliced
2   tablespoons roasted red pepper, diced
    No Oil Raspberry Vinaigrette (See Index)

1. Prepare all vegetables.

2. Place in a bowl and add enough dressing to coat (not drench) vegetables and beans. Toss gently. Serve at room temperature.

Serving:	1
Calories:	160
Fat grams:	1.0
% of Fat:	3%

WINTER BEET SALAD

(serves 4)

6   heads of Belgian endive, trimmed
3   large beets
    Lemon Dijon Dressing (See Index)

1. Cut off beet greens (can be steamed with other vegetables if used right away), leaving a couple of inches attached to beets. Rinse. Place in large pot of boiling water and cook for 40–50 minutes, depending on size.

2. Rinse in cold water and slip off skins.

3. Slice beets; cut in halves and place in a bowl. Let cool.

4. Separate endive leaves and soak for 5 minutes in salted ice water to remove bitterness. Drain and pat dry. Cut into 1" segments.

5. Place endive on individual plates. Place beets on top. Drizzle dressing on top of beets. Serve chilled.

Serving:	1
Calories:	140
Fat grams:	2.0
% of Fat:	10%

Side Dishes

5

ARROZ MEXICANA

(serves 6)

1   quart water
2   tablespoons vegetable chicken-style broth powder
½   onion, minced
4   large cloves garlic, minced
2   cups long grain brown rice, washed but uncooked
½   green pepper, cut into thin strips
2   tomatoes, seeded and chopped
¼   cup dry white wine
½   teaspoon saffron threads (or turmeric)
1   cup peas
    Sea salt, to taste
    Freshly ground black pepper, to taste

1. Bring water and vegetable broth powder to a boil.

2. Sauté onion and garlic in water or vegetable stock in a large, heavy bottomed, lidded pot or casserole dish. When onion is soft, add uncooked rice, stirring for 1 minute.

3. Add peppers and tomatoes and stir together for a couple of minutes.

4. Add wine and continue to stir until liquid has been absorbed.

5. Add simmering stock and saffron, bring to a slow boil over medium heat, and cook for 25 minutes.

6. Add peas and continue to cook until all liquid is absorbed or until rice is cooked *al dente* and peas are cooked through, about 10 more minutes.

7. Pour off any stock that remains, add salt and pepper to taste.

'Freezer Friendly'

Serving:	1
Calories:	285
Fat grams:	2.5
% of Fat:	7%

BAKED FRENCH FRIES

(serves 4)

Potatoes, preferably organic
Spike (optional)
Garlic powder (optional)
Paprika (optional)
Chili powder (optional)

1. Preheat oven to 450 degrees.

2. Scrub potatoes; no need to peel. Slice into desired size and shape. Place "fries" on a nonstick, lightly oiled cookie sheet.

3. Bake 30–40 minutes, depending on size of potato slices.

4. When removing, use turned over spatula to scrape free of sheet. Serve hot, alone or with ketchup.

Helpful Hints

Soaking potato slices in cold water for ½ hour or so before baking makes for "lighter" french fries.

Use yams the same way as potatoes for delicious "yam fries," which require less time to bake.

Serving:	½ potato
Calories:	245
Fat grams:	0
% of Fat:	1%

BEETS IN CITRUS DRESSING

(serves 4)

Serve as a side dish with any of the loaf recipes.

3	medium beets
½	cup fresh orange juice
1	tablespoon lemon juice
⅛	teaspoon ground cloves
	Pinch of salt
	Pinch of freshly ground black pepper
	Pinch of guar gum (optional, to thicken)

1. Cut off beet greens (can be steamed with other vegetables, if used right away), leaving a couple of inches attached to beets. Rinse. Place in large pot of boiling water and cook for 40–50 minutes, depending on size.

2. Rinse in cold water and slip off skins.

3. Slice beets and cut in halves and place in a bowl.

4. Mix together orange and lemon juice, with ground cloves, salt and pepper (and guar gum, if used), in a blender.

5. Pour dressing over beets, mix gently.

Serving:	1
Calories:	40
Fat grams:	0
% of Fat:	3%

BROCCOLI & CAULIFLOWER MELANGE

(serves 4)

1   head broccoli, cut into florets
½   head cauliflower, cut into florets
½   cup roasted red pepper, diced
8–10 button mushrooms, whole
     Spicy Orange Sauce (See Index)

1. Steam vegetables except the red pepper for 5–6 minutes until tender crisp.

2. Toss with red pepper and enough dressing to coat, not drench. Serve hot.

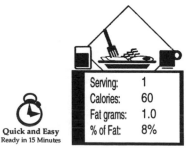

Quick and Easy
Ready in 15 Minutes

Serving:	1
Calories:	60
Fat grams:	1.0
% of Fat:	8%

BROCCOLI WITH CURRY SAUCE

(serves 4)

1   head broccoli, cut lengthwise with approximately 3"
      of the spear attached
4   cherry tomatoes
      Curry Sauce (See Index)

1. Cut off tough part of the broccoli stalks, leaving approximately 3 inches of the stalk.

2. Prepare Curry Sauce as per instructions.

3. Steam broccoli for 6 minutes until tender crisp.

4. Place broccoli on individual plates; pour ¼ cup of hot sauce over broccoli. Place a cherry tomato on the side for garnish.

Option

Asparagus in season can be substituted beautifully.

Quick and Easy
Ready in 15 Minutes

Serving:	1
Calories:	50
Fat grams:	0
% of Fat:	7%

CANDIED YAMS

(makes 3 quarts)

3   quarts yams (4 lbs.)
1¼ cups raisins
1   20 ounce can unsweetened crushed pineapple, with
     juice
1   tablespoon Sucanat
2   cups apple juice
2   cups slivered and blanched almonds (optional)
1   teaspoon cinnamon, to taste
½   teaspoon nutmeg, to taste

1. Peel and cube yams.

2. Steam yam cubes until partially cooked, but not mushy.

3. Combine all ingredients and place in a casserole dish.

4. Bake uncovered at 400 degrees for 40–45 minutes.

Serving:	1 cup
Calories:	250
Fat grams:	1.0
% of Fat:	2%

BROWN RICE WITH CARAWAY SEEDS

(serves 4)

Serve as a salad with vegetables or as a side dish.

⅔ cup long grain brown rice
⅓ cup rye berries
1½ teaspoon caraway seeds (½ teaspoon per cup)

1. No matter what quantity of rice you choose to make, use this ratio.

2. Cook in your usual method.

Serving:	1
Calories:	130
Fat grams:	1.0
% of Fat:	7%

CORNBREAD LOAF

(makes 2 loaves; serves 12)

Spread with your favorite natural preserves.

4   cups fine cornmeal
2   cups whole wheat pastry flour
¾   cup millet, soak in boiling hot water; drain
1   teaspoon sea salt
1½ tablespoons baking powder
1   cup applesauce
¾   cup honey
2   teaspoons rice vinegar
3   cups "lite" soy milk, plain

1. Place all dry ingredients in large mixing bowl. Stir to combine.

2. Blend applesauce, honey, vinegar and soy milk in a blender or food processor.

3. Pour wet ingredients into dry, mixing well, approximately 2 minutes.

4. Pour into 2 lightly oiled loaf pans. Bake for 1 hour at 350 degrees. Check with a toothpick to see if batter is cooked; if toothpick comes out with batter, lower oven to 300 degrees and continue to cook until done. Check every 10 minutes after first hour has passed.

5. Remove from oven and let cool for 10 minutes. Then de-loaf.

Option

Substitute rice flour for whole wheat pastry flour; or use 1 cup rice flour and 1 cup whole wheat pastry flour.

'Freezer Friendly'

Serving:	1
Calories:	270
Fat grams:	2.0
% of Fat:	3%

CREAMED CORN POLENTA

(serves 6)

½   onion, chopped
½   red pepper, chopped
2   jalapeno chilies, chopped
¼   cup pimentos, chopped (optional)
3   cups water
3   tablespoons vegetable chicken-style broth powder
1   cup corn (if frozen, defrost before blending)
1¼ cup coarse polenta
½   cup "lite" soy milk
½   teaspoon salt

1. Sauté onion, red pepper and jalapeno in a little water, until onion is translucent.

2. Add water and vegetable broth and bring to a boil.

3. Mix corn and soy milk in a blender until creamy.

4. Add creamed corn to water, broth and vegetables.

5. Slowly add polenta to simmering liquid, stirring constantly until polenta starts to thicken.

6. Pour cooked polenta into a pyrex dish, small molds or any dish that will lend itself to cutting polenta into squares or slices after it has set.

7. Allow polenta to set for at least 45 minutes. Slice as a side dish or main course.

Serving:	1
Calories:	160
Fat grams:	1.5
% of Fat:	9%

CURRIED CAULIFLOWER & CARROTS

(serves 4)

1   medium cauliflower, cut into florets
2   cups carrots, crinkle sliced ¼" pieces
1   red pepper, diced
     Apple juice, as needed
     Curry Sauce (See Index)

1. Sauté carrots in apple juice until nearly tender. Add red pepper and continue cooking until tender crisp.

2. While carrots are sautéing, steam cauliflower 5–6 minutes until tender crisp.

3. Toss vegetables together with enough sauce to coat, not drench. Serve hot.

Option

Add ½ cup raisins to carrots and red pepper while cooking.

Serving:	1
Calories:	75
Fat grams:	0
% of Fat:	4%

GINGERED CARROTS

(makes 1 quart; serves 4)

6   large carrots (1¼ lbs.), crinkle cut
1   tablespoon ginger root, grated or pureed
½   orange rind, grated (orange part only)
1   tablespoon honey
     Arrowroot, as required (dissolved in water)
     Fresh parsley, for garnish

1. Cook carrots in ½" water, covered, until tender (about 15 minutes).

2. Add ginger, orange rind and honey. Stir well.

3. Remove carrots.

4. Taste carrot sauce and adjust as required, to taste. Then add arrowroot, dissolved in water, to thicken mixture.

5. Return carrots to thickened mixture; stir. Garnish with fresh parsley sprigs. Serve hot.

Helpful Hint

For a more flavorful sauce, use carrot juice to cook the carrots.

'Freezer Friendly'

Serving:	1
Calories:	65
Fat grams:	0
% of Fat:	3%

MEDITERRANEAN GREEN BEANS

(serves 2)

½ tablespoons red wine vinegar (or Balsamic vinegar)
½ teaspoon Dijon mustard
1 clove garlic, pressed
¼ teaspoon oregano (or ½ teaspoon fresh)
⅛ teaspoon freshly ground black pepper
½ lb. green beans, trimmed

1. Steam green beans, either whole or sliced in half, diagonally.

2. Whisk vinegar, mustard, garlic, oregano and pepper in a large bowl.

3. Add cooked beans and toss to coat. Serve hot or at room temperature.

Quick and Easy
Ready in 15 Minutes

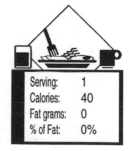

Serving:	1
Calories:	40
Fat grams:	0
% of Fat:	0%

POTATO BOATS

(serves 4)

2   large Idaho or russet potatoes
1   lb. banana squash, approximately ½–¾ cup*
⅛   teaspoon curry or cumin
½   teaspoon Spike (optional)
     Paprika, for garnish

1. Bake potatoes at 450 degrees until soft, about 60 minutes (depending upon size of potatoes).

2. While potatoes are baking, cut and peel squash. Cut squash into small cubes and steam until very soft.

3. While potatoes are still hot, cut them in half and, using a pot holder to hold each potato, gently scrape pulp from skin, taking care not to tear skin. (This process should allow the potato skin to remain firm, if not crisp.)

4. Combine squash, potato pulp, cumin, and Spike using a potato masher or food processor until you have a creamy yellow puree. (Add water or vegetable stock to moisten if necessary.) *Do not over process!*

5. Spoon potato-squash mixture into empty potato shells. Use a fork to decorate the top of the filling.

6. Sprinkle with paprika. Place under broiler for 10 minutes until lightly browned.

*When cooking more potatoes, use a 2 to 1 ratio; 2 parts potato to 1 part squash.

Serving:	1
Calories:	120
Fat grams:	0
% of Fat:	0%

BABY RED POTATOES DIJON

(serves 6)

12 small red potatoes
    Dijon mustard

1. Steam potatoes for about 20 minutes; then plunge into cold water. Chill.

2. Slice each potato in half; scoop out a small hole in the center of each half.

3. Fill each hole with mustard and garnish with paprika and a bit of roasted red pepper or pimento.

Serving:	1
Calories:	90
Fat grams:	0
% of Fat:	0%

RICE MEDLEY

(makes 3 cups; serves 4)

Rice can be refrigerated or frozen.

    2   cups vegetable stock
         Dash of tamari
    ½   cup carrots, finely diced
    3   cloves garlic, minced
    2   scallions, finely sliced
    1   small stalk celery, finely chopped
    1   cup rice, as follows: 1 tablespoon each of rye berries,
         wheat berries, wild rice, and millet. Top off with long-
         grain brown rice, heaping full

1. Add vegetables to stock, bring to a boil and simmer for 5–10 minutes.

2. Add rice mixture and stir. Lower heat to medium and cover. After 10 minutes, lower heat to the lowest setting and let cook for 50 minutes. Do not lift cover until done, then turn off and let set for 5 minutes. Stir and mix all ingredients. This recipe can be doubled or tripled.

'Freezer Friendly'

Serving:	1
Calories:	240
Fat grams:	1.5
% of Fat:	6%

ROSEMARY MASHED POTATOES

(serves 6)

Serve hot as a side dish or entrée. Top with Savory Mushroom or Country Style Gravy (See Index).

    8   medium potatoes, peeled and quartered
    ½   teaspoon rosemary powder, to taste*
        Salt, to taste
        Fresh white pepper, to taste

1. Cook potatoes until falling apart, approximately 20 plus minutes. Drain, reserving cooking water.

2. In a large bowl, mash cooked potatoes, adding enough cooking liquid to make smooth.

4. Add rosemary, salt and pepper, to taste.

Powdered rosemary can be made by grinding dried rosemary in a coffee grinder, mortar and pestle, or a Japanese suribachi .

Helpful Hint

You may use soy milk instead of the cooking water, however, it makes the potatoes richer (higher fat).

Serving:	1
Calories:	120
Fat grams:	0
% of Fat:	0%

ROASTED POTATOES

(serves 4)

2   lbs. new potatoes, unpeeled
10 large cloves garlic, crushed
¼   cup fresh rosemary, finely chopped (or 3 tablespoons dried, crushed in mortar)
½   cup stock or water
    Sea salt, to taste
    Freshly ground black pepper, to taste

1. Preheat oven to 375 degrees.

2. Wash potatoes and cut into quarters. Place in a baking dish with garlic cloves and stock or water.

3. Sprinkle with rosemary and toss.

4. Cover and bake for 30 minutes, then remove cover and roast for another 30–40 minutes until done. Additional stock or water may be necessary.

5. Stir gently, mixing the herbs, garlic and stock, occasionally.

6. Add salt and pepper, to taste. Serve hot.

Serving:	1
Calories:	170
Fat grams:	0
% of Fat:	0%

SWISS CHARD WITH GINGER

(serves 4)

2   shallots, sliced
1   tablespoon ginger, minced
1   jalapeno pepper, finely minced
1   bunch swiss chard, washed, cut into 1" pieces
     Salt & fresh black pepper, to taste

1. Saute the shallots, ginger and pepper for a few minutes in a dash of stock or water.

2. Place chard evenly on top, and cover.

3. Steam for 4-5 minutes until tender. Salt and pepper to taste.

Serving:	1
Calories:	20
Fat grams:	0
% of Fat:	5

WILD RICE PILAF

(makes 6¾ cups; serves 6)

2   cloves garlic, minced
1   cup onion, finely diced
2   tablespoons fresh ginger, grated
½   teaspoon black pepper
½   cup wild rice
1½ cups long grain brown rice
4   cups stock or water
2   tablespoons tamari (optional)

1. Sauté garlic, onion and ginger in ½ cup water for 5 minutes.

2. Add pepper, wild rice and brown rice and sauté for 3–5 minutes.

3. Add stock or water, and tamari, if desired.

4. Boil for 10 minutes, covered. Lower to a simmer, over low heat, and continue to cook for 45 minutes.

5. Let rest for 15 minutes.

Option

Prepare in an electric rice cooker, same as above except reduce stock or water to 2½ cups. Measure rice and wild rice; wash and drain. Combine rices with onion, garlic, ginger, pepper and tamari. Stir well. Place in rice cooker with 2½ cups stock or water. Soak for ½ hour. Cook and let rest for 15 minutes. Remove from cooker and stir to fluff.

'Freezer Friendly'

Serving:	1
Calories:	190
Fat grams:	1.5
% of Fat:	5%

YAMS Á L'ORANGE

(serves 8)

4   fat garnet yams, approximately 4 lbs.
1   jar orange marmalade (fruit sweetened)

1. Wash yams, slice off ends.

2. Slice yams ¾" thick. Place on lightly oiled baking dish (pyrex or baked enamel).

3. Bake covered for 30 minutes at 350 degrees.

4. Uncover and place one heaping teaspoon of marmalade on each slice.

5. Recover and place back in oven for 15 minutes, or until yams are tender. Serve hot.

Serving:	1
Calories:	345
Fat grams:	0
% of Fat:	1%

Soups

6

ASPARAGUS SOUP

(serves 4)

1   cup medium potatoes, peeled and cubed
½   cup onions, chopped
2   cups stock or water
1½ lbs. fresh asparagus, cut in 2–3" pieces
4   ribs celery stalks with tops, chopped
2   tablespoons whole wheat flour
     Freshly ground black pepper, to taste
½   teaspoon marjoram
½   teaspoon tarragon
1   teaspoon Spike (optional)
1   teaspoon tamari
1   teaspoon Herbamare
1   cup cashew milk*
2   teaspoons minced chives

1. Cook potatoes and onion in water or stock for 15–20 minutes.

2. Add remaining ingredients, except cashew milk. Bring to a boil.

3. Cover and simmer 20–30 minutes or until asparagus is tender.

4. Stir in cashew milk; continue cooking 5 minutes.

5. Garnish with minced chives. Serve hot or cold.

*Mix 1/4 cup cashews and enough water to make 1 cup. Blend until creamy, add arrowroot and blend until smooth.

Helpful Hints

Before adding cashew milk, puree soup in blender for 20 seconds. Return to pan and proceed as above.

If you are using stock, make the stock in your usual way, but add the tough parts of the asparagus which you usually discard. This gives a stronger asparagus flavor.

Serving:	1
Calories:	144
Fat grams:	4.5
% of Fat:	25%

CHERRY BORSCHT

(serves 4)

28 ounces vegetable beef-style stock
2–3 sticks cinnamon
1   lb. canned pickled beets, well drained with liquid
      reserved, chopped
2   tablespoons Sucanat
1   lb. fresh or frozen bing cherries, washed, stemmed,
      pitted
      Lemon juice, to taste
      Tofu Sour Cream (See Index)

1. Bring beef-style stock to a boil with cinnamon sticks.

2. Add chopped beets, beet liquid and Sucanat.

3. Heat until boiling again; then add cherries and quickly return to a boil.

4. Remove cinnamon sticks if flavor is strong enough, or leave in for more flavor.

5. Cover the soup and chill thoroughly. Add a little lemon juice if too sweet. Garnish each bowl with a spoonful of Tofu Sour Cream. Serve chilled.

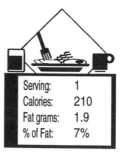

Serving:	1
Calories:	210
Fat grams:	1.9
% of Fat:	7%

BEAN SOUP DU JOUR

(makes 6½ quarts)

6 cups dry beans, assorted
2 gallons water
1 large carrot, rough chopped
2 large onions, rough chopped
1 celery stalk, rough chopped
10 cloves whole garlic
2 potatoes, peeled and quartered
5 bay leaves
3 sprigs rosemary (or 2 tablespoons dried)
   Salt & freshly ground black pepper, to taste

1. Sort and soak beans overnight. Discard soaking water. Rinse and add 2 gallons of fresh water. Add all vegetables except potato; bring to a boil and simmer, covered, for 1 ½ hours.

2. Add potatoes and simmer for another ½ hour. Turn heat off and let sit for ½ to 1 hour.

3. Remove most of the beans and vegetables. Discard vegetables and save the beans. You may freeze some, if you wish, for other dishes.

4. Ladle some of the beans and the liquid into a blender or food processor and puree. Return soup to the pot.

5. Season to your taste.

Helpful Hints

The seasonings are your option. Use your favorite fresh or dried herbs. Try using tabasco. Add pasta to the soup for a hearty winter meal, served with crusty bread.

Options

Beans	Spices
2 cups kidney	1 tablespoon salt
2 cups pinto	1 teaspoon fresh black pepper
1 cup anasazi	1 teaspoon tabasco
1 cup black	

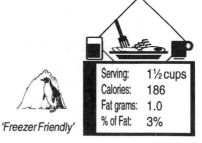

'Freezer Friendly'

Serving:	1½ cups
Calories:	186
Fat grams:	1.0
% of Fat:	3%

BLACK BEAN SOUP

(makes 4 quarts)

2   cups black beans, dry
1   bay leaf
12   cups vegetable stock
1½   cups onions, diced
1   tablespoon garlic, minced
2   teaspoons cumin
6   ounces tomato paste
1   cup carrots, thinly sliced
1   teaspoon coriander
1   teaspoon sage
½   teaspoon cayenne
1   teaspoon sea salt
½   teaspoon freshly ground black pepper
     Bragg Liquid Aminos, to taste
½   cup dry sherry

1. Sort and soak beans overnight in three times their volume of water.

2. Drain beans, discarding soaking water, and cover again with three times the volume of fresh water. Bring to a boil, add bay leaf, lower heat and simmer for one hour.

3. While beans are cooking, heat a small amount of stock; add onions, garlic and cumin. Stir frequently until onions are translucent.

4. Mix in tomato paste. Add carrots and continue cooking an additional 10 minutes.

5. Drain partially cooked beans. Add to sautéed mixture. Stir to coat.

6. Add 12 cups of stock. Bring to a boil. Add coriander, sage and cayenne. Let simmer until beans are tender, approximately one more hour.

7. Add Bragg, sherry and pepper, and cook for another 20 minutes. Add salt.

8. Place half the soup in a food processor and make a thick puree. Return soup back to the pot and stir.

Serving:	1½ cups
Calories:	254
Fat grams:	1.2
% of Fat:	4%

CORN & GREEN CHILI CHOWDER

(serves 6)

3½ cups "lite" soy milk
1¼ cups onion, diced
1   bay leaf
4   branches parsley
1   branch fresh thyme
1   4" branch marjoram
8   peppercorns
3   poblano or anaheim chilies (or 1 large bell pepper)
8   ounces tomatillo
5   cups yellow corn
1   cup water
2   tablespoons stock
½   teaspoon salt
     Cilantro leaves, coarsely chopped for garnish

1. Slowly heat soy milk with half the diced onion and bay leaf, parsley, thyme, marjoram and peppercorns. Just before it comes to a boil, turn off the heat and cover.

2. Let soy milk steep with the herbs.

3. Roast chilies or bell pepper over a flame until the skins blister and char. Place them in a bowl, cover with a dish, and set them aside to steam for 10 minutes.

4. Bring several cups of water to a boil, then lower heat to a simmer. Remove papery husks from the tomatillos, rinse and drop tomatillos into simmering water to cook slowly for 10 minutes.

5. Puree cooked tomatillos in a blender. (If using canned tomatillos, drain first, then puree.)

6. Set aside 1 cup of corn kernels. Blend the remainder in two batches with 1 cup of water at the highest speed for 2 minutes.

7. Work corn puree through a fine meshed sieve to press out all the liquid.

8. Heat stock in a soup pot with a little water. Add remaining onion and cook over medium-low heat until soft.

9. Add pureed tomatillos, corn kernels, peppers and salt.

10. Cook for 2–3 minutes, then stir in pureed corn and strained milk.

11. Cook the soup over low heat for about 30 minutes, stirring frequently. Check the seasonings and add salt, if necessary. Garnish with cilantro.

Serving:	1
Calories:	184
Fat grams:	4.7
% of Fat:	20%

FRESH CORN GAZPACHO

(makes 5 cups)

2	cups frozen corn, rinsed
4	small pickling cucumbers, peeled, cubed
½	green or red pepper, diced
3	scallions, finely sliced
2	jalapeno peppers, finely diced
1	28 ounce can stewed tomatoes, pureed in blender
4	cups peeled tomato pieces, with juice
3	tablespoons fresh lemon juice
1½	teaspoons ground cumin
1	clove garlic, minced
1	teaspoon salt

1. Rinse corn. Cook in boiling water or steam just until tender and drain well.

2. Combine all ingredients.

3. Refrigerate 12 to 24 hours. Serve very cold.

Option

Mix in 2 tablespoons fresh chopped cilantro, sliced radishes or small yellow tomatoes.

Serving:	1¼ cups
Calories:	194
Fat grams:	1.1
% of Fat:	4%

CREAMY YAM SOUP

(makes 2 quarts; serves 6)

5   cups stock or water
8   cups yams, peeled, chopped
2   large carrots, peeled, roughly chopped
2   large celery stalks, roughly chopped
1½ cups fresh or frozen corn (if frozen, rinse)
½   teaspoon cinnamon
¼   teaspoon ground ginger
½   teaspoon salt

1. Bring stock or water to a boil.

2. Add all ingredients except corn.

3. Boil until all vegetables are soft, approximately 30 minutes.

4. Place in a blender or food processor and blend until smooth.

5. Return to pot, add corn, and keep warm on low heat for 15 minutes.

Serving:	1
Calories:	366
Fat grams:	1.3
% of Fat:	3%

FRENCH ONION SOUP

(serves 6)

Serve in soup bowls and top each with ½ teaspoon of nutritional yeast.

2   lbs. onions, french cut, quartered
2   tablespoons whole wheat pastry flour
⅛   teaspoon cumin
6   cups water
¼   cup vegetarian beef-style broth powder
5   tablespoons miso, traditional
1   tablespoon tamari
1   teaspoon worcestershire (without anchovies)
1   tablespoon onion powder
     Dash freshly ground black pepper
     Nutritional yeast

   1. Sauté onions in stock or water to lightly caramelize. This could take 20–25 minutes, but is well worth it as the caramelizing adds a rich, sweet flavor. Add liquid while caramelizing.

   2. Add flour and cumin; stir to coat onions.

   3. Combine water and remaining ingredients. Bring to a boil and add onion mixture.

   4. Simmer until onions are cooked.

'Freezer Friendly'

Serving:	1
Calories:	110
Fat grams:	1.5
% of Fat:	11%

MINESTRONE SOUP

(makes 2½ quarts)

1   cup dried kidney beans
½   teaspoon crushed garlic
1½ cups onion, chopped
1   stalk celery, sliced
1   carrot, sliced
1   potato, chopped
1   cup string beans, sliced in 1" pieces
1   cup tomato sauce
1   cup tomato pieces
2   tablespoons parsley
¼   teaspoon celery seed
½   teaspoon marjoram
1½ teaspoons basil
1½ teaspoons oregano
¼   teaspoon freshly ground black pepper
1   zucchini, diced
1   cup cabbage, shredded
½   cup whole wheat elbow macaroni
1   quart bean water
1   tablespoon dark miso

1. Sort and soak beans overnight in three times the volume of water. Drain beans, discarding soaking water, then cook beans again in enough water to more than cover.

2. Sauté onions and garlic in bean water for 20 minutes to make a rich stock.

3. Add celery, carrots, potatoes and green beans. Cook each vegetable 3 minutes before adding the next. Add cooked beans and all the seasonings.

4. After 30 minutes, add zucchini and miso. Cook another 30 minutes; add cabbage, macaroni, tomato sauce and tomatoes. Simmer for another 20–30 minutes. Adjust seasonings.

'Freezer Friendly'

Serving:	1½ cups
Calories:	180
Fat grams:	1.0
% of Fat:	4%

HOT AND SOUR SOUP

(serves 4)

⅓ to ½ cup vegetarian chicken-style broth powder
1   quart water
10   slices fresh ginger
½   cup slivered seitan
½   cup carrots, julienne
½   cup napa cabbage, julienne
½   cup dried black mushroom slices, soaked, drained*
½   cup sliced dried lily flower buds, soaked, drained*
½   cup frozen baby peas, rinsed, thawed
4   scallions, whites thinly sliced; greens cut in thin
     diagonals and 2 kept separate
2   tablespoons rice vinegar (unseasoned)
1   tablespoon mirin
2   tablespoons tamari
½   teaspoon freshly ground black pepper
1½   tablespoons arrowroot
⅛   teaspoon + crushed red pepper, to taste

1. Cut and prepare all fresh and dried vegetables and seitan.

2. After soaking and draining black mushrooms and lily flowers, slice them so they are not too stringy.

3. Simmer broth powder, water and ginger for one minute, then remove the ginger.

4. Combine rice vinegar, mirin, tamari, black pepper, arrowroot and red pepper in a bowl and mix.

5. Add carrots, napa cabbage and black mushrooms to stock and simmer for 2 minutes.

6. Add remaining ingredients except the scallion greens and baby peas, and simmer another 2 minutes. Be sure to mix the mixture in the bowl to recirculate the arrowroot before adding to the soup.

7. Add baby peas; adjust the seasonings. Garnish with scallion greens. Serve very hot.

available only at your Asian grocery store.

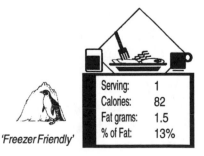

'Freezer Friendly'

Serving:	1
Calories:	82
Fat grams:	1.5
% of Fat:	13%

MOROCCAN CHICKPEA SOUP

(makes 4 quarts)

1   cup dry garbanzo beans (chickpeas)
¾   cup red lentils
1¼   cups red onion, finely diced
1½   cups celery, finely diced
12   cups stock or water
12   ounces tomato paste
½   cup miso, light mellow
2   teaspoons ground coriander
1   tablespoon basil
2   cups zucchini, sliced
½   cup fresh parsley, finely chopped
       Dash of white pepper
2   tablespoons lemon juice
½   cup elbow pasta, soy or wheat, or spaghetti

1. Sort through and wash garbanzo beans; soak overnight in three times the volume of water. Discard soaking water. Rinse and cover again with three times the volume of water. Cook until tender, approximately 2 ½ hours; then drain.

2. Sauté cooked garbanzo beans, raw lentils, red onion and celery in one cup stock or water, until celery is translucent, approximately 5 minutes.

3. Add tomato paste and miso, mixing well into bean and vegetable mixture.

4. Add remaining stock or water and bring to a simmer.

5. Add pasta, zucchini, parsley, coriander, basil and pepper. Cook until zucchini is tender and pasta breaks down, thickening soup, approximately 25 minutes.

6. Add lemon juice and adjust seasonings to taste.

'Freezer Friendly'

Serving:	1½ cups
Calories:	370
Fat grams:	2.7
% of Fat:	6%

MUSHROOM BARLEY SOUP

(makes 3 quarts)

8	cups stock or water
1	potato, diced
2	stalks celery, diced
½	cup cabbage, chopped
1	onion, diced
2	cloves garlic, minced
½	lb. mushrooms, sliced
2	carrots, diced
½	cup tomato puree
¼	cup sun-dried tomato, soaked, chopped
¼	cup split peas
½	cup barley
1	teaspoon sea salt
½	teaspoon freshly ground black pepper
	Fresh parsley

1. Combine all ingredients; bring to a boil. Reduce heat and simmer 1½ hours. Garnish with parsley.

Serving:	1½ cups
Calories:	200
Fat grams:	1.0
% of Fat:	4%

POTATO LEEK SOUP

(makes 5 quarts)

3   medium onions, chopped
5   ribs celery, sliced
9   cups stock
4   bay leaves (bag in cheesecloth)
1   tablespoon Touch of Herbs (See Index)
1½ teaspoon basil
4   large leeks (white and green portion, sliced)*
5   medium potatoes, peeled, chunked
2   medium potatoes, peeled, ½" diced
⅓   cup chives, dried or fresh
5   tablespoons white miso
½   teaspoon salt
¼   teaspoon white pepper

1. Sauté onion and celery in some stock or water.

2. Add stock, chunked potatoes, bay leaves, Touch of Herbs and basil; simmer until vegetables are tender.

3. Puree all cooked vegetables in a blender or food processor.

4. Sauté leeks; cut in half, quartered and sliced.

5. Boil potatoes, peeled and diced ½", until firm; drain.

6. Combine sautéed leeks, boiled diced potatoes and pureed mixture.

7. Add chopped chives, miso, salt and white pepper to sautéed soup.

Slice leeks in half, then quarters. Wash thoroughly:
  then slice and wash again.

Serving:	1½ cups
Calories:	224
Fat grams:	1.0
% of Fat:	4%

SPICY TOMATO SOUP

(makes 5 quarts)

½   lb onions, finely diced
1   ounce garlic, minced
4   quarts tomato juice
2   teaspoons tabasco sauce, to taste
½   cup salsa
2   teaspoons chili powder
1½ ounces vegetable chicken-style broth powder
2   ounces miso
    Freshly ground black pepper, to taste
4   ounces farina
1   teaspoon potato starch
1   quart cooked long grain brown rice
    Salt, to taste*

1. Sauté onion and garlic in small amount of tomato juice.

2. Mix farina and potato starch with two times the volume of cold tomato juice; set aside for later use.

3. Add tomato juice, salsa, chili powder, vegetable broth powder and miso to sautéed onion and garlic and simmer 15 minutes. *Stir often! Be careful not to burn!*

4. Add cooked rice.

5. Add tabasco. *Be careful not to make too hot!*

6. Depending on how thick the soup becomes with the addition of rice, add reserved farina and tomato juice mixture gradually, stirring constantly. *Be careful not to make too thick!* Serve hot or cold.

Salt may not be needed at all, depending on the salt content of the tomato juice.

'Freezer Friendly'

Serving:	1½ cups
Calories:	146
Fat grams:	1.0
% of Fat:	6%

VEGETABLE STOCK

(makes 12 quarts)

1	large parsnip
1	large turnip
2+	large onions
2+	large carrots
2+	celery stalks, including plenty of leaves
¼	bunch parsley
1	large potato (peelings will do fine)
1	corn cob (or whole ear)
	Squash seeds, if available
	Pea pods, if available
1	broccoli stalk, cut up
1	teaspoon peppercorns
2	bay leaves
2	cloves garlic
	Assorted herbs
1	teaspoon basil
½	teaspoon celery seed
	Mushroom bits, if available
	Scallion greens, if available
	Zucchini ends, if available
1 or 2	lettuce leaves (outer)

1. Always use firm, fresh vegetables, or wash and store them in a snap lock storage bag in the freezer.

2. Wash and scrub all vegetables and trim off ends. Cut into 2–4 inch pieces; the more surface of the vegetables, the more flavor.

3. Sauté in water all small vegetables in the bottom of the pot, adding garlic and herbs, until the vegetables "sweat."

4. Add enough water to cover, and bring to a boil. Add water until desired amount of stock is reached. Reduce to a simmer and continue simmering for an hour or more, until all of the flavors have had a chance to come out.

5. Remove larger vegetables with a chinois or a strainer. Strain stock through a strainer. The best method is to use a cheesecloth for the final straining.

6. For a richer stock, continue to reduce by simmering after vegetables have been removed.

7. When stock is complete and strained, place entire pot in a sink filled with cold water (adding ice will cool it down even faster).

8. Place in the refrigerator, with a large spoon upside down under the pot to allow cold air to circulate.

9. Do not cover until stock is cool.

10. Freeze small and large containers of stock, so you always have some on hand. Fill ice cube trays with stock; when they are frozen, pop them into a snap lock storage bag and use them for sautéing.

Option

If you do not have a large enough pot, cut the ingredients in half.

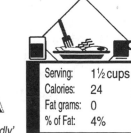

'Freezer Friendly'

Serving:	1½ cups
Calories:	24
Fat grams:	0
% of Fat:	4%

SPICY CORN & CHICKPEA SOUP WITH CHILIES

(makes 10 cups)

½   cup dry garbanzo beans (chickpeas)
1   quart cold water
1   bay leaf
2   fresh sage leaves
1   fresh marjoram sprig
1   tablespoon stock
2   cups onion, diced
     Sea salt, to taste
1½ teaspoon cumin, toasted
½   teaspoon oregano, toasted
     Pinch cayenne pepper
6   cloves garlic, minced
1   cup yellow bell pepper, diced
2   cups corn
½   cup canned hominy
28   ounce can tomatoes, diced with juice
⅛   teaspoon Liquid Smoke
2   green jalapeno chilies, seeded, coarsely chopped
     and pureed with ½ cup water
2   tablespoons lime juice
1   tablespoon fresh sage, chopped
     Sucanat
3   tablespoons cilantro, chopped

1. Sort and soak garbanzo beans overnight. Drain and rinse, discarding soaking water. Place beans in a pot with water, bay leaf, sage leaves and marjoram. Bring to a boil, then reduce heat and simmer, uncovered, until beans are tender, 40–50 minutes. Remove herbs and leave beans in their broth.

2. Heat stock over medium heat in a soup pot and add onions, ½ teaspoon salt, toasted cumin and oregano, and a pinch of cayenne pepper.

3. Sauté until onions are translucent, about 7–8 minutes, then add garlic, peppers, corn and hominy.

4. Cook vegetables for 5 minutes, then add tomatoes, 1 teaspoon salt and the garbanzo beans in their broth.

5. Season soup to taste with Liquid Smoke flavoring and jalapeno puree. *Be careful not to make the soup too hot!*

6. Add lime juice, sage and ½ teaspoon salt. Add a few pinches of Sucanat. Cover and cook over low heat for 30 minutes.

7. Stir in cilantro just before serving.

Serving:	1½ cups
Calories:	180
Fat grams:	2.3
% of Fat:	10%

SUCCOTASH CHOWDER

(makes 4 quarts)

1   cup stock or water
3   cups onion, diced
3   cups celery, finely diced
3   large cloves garlic, finely minced
1   cup scallions, sliced
1   cup parsnip, peeled, diced
2   tablespoons basil
1   tablespoon thyme
    Several sprigs fresh dill, finely chopped (or ½
    teaspoon dried)
2½ cups dry baby lima beans
16 cups corn
10 cups "lite" soy milk
¼   cup fresh parsley, finely chopped
¼   cup tamari
    Spike or sea salt, to taste
    Fresh ground white pepper, to taste
3   scallions, thinly sliced

1. Sort, wash and soak beans overnight in three times the volume of water. Drain, discarding soaking water, and cover again with three times the volume of water. Cook approximately 1½ hours. Cook until just tender, *not* to the point of falling apart.

2. Heat stock, onions, celery and garlic over medium heat in a large stock pot. Stir often and cook 2–3 minutes.

3. Add parsnips and cook another 5 minutes. Add basil, thyme and dill, stirring for 15 seconds.

4. Add drained cooked lima beans and corn. Stir, coating with the herb mixture.

5. Add warmed or room temperature soy milk (for thinner soup, add extra water), parsley and tamari. Cook approximately 30 minutes.

6. Season to taste with Spike or salt and pepper. Garnish with scallions. Serve hot or warm.

Serving:	1½ cups
Calories:	492
Fat grams:	8.1
% of Fat:	14%

TUSCAN BEAN SOUP

(makes 10 quarts)

1	lb. onion, diced
3	cloves garlic, minced
1	lb. celery, diced
1	lb. carrots, diced
2	lbs. potatoes, peeled, diced
1	lb. cabbage, chopped
1	quart tomato pieces, drained
4	quarts vegetable stock
1	teaspoon crushed red pepper
1	tablespoon thyme
1	tablespoon salt
1	teaspoon Liquid Smoke
4	quarts cooked white beans *Do not drain after cooking*
2	tablespoons tamari
¼	cup worcestershire sauce (without anchovies)

1. Sort and soak beans overnight; drain, discarding soaking water, and cook in water 2½ times their original volume. Reserve cooking liquid.

2. Sauté onion and garlic in 1½ cups stock.

3. Add diced celery and carrots, and continue sautéing about 15 minutes. Add stock, if necessary.

4. Add diced potatoes, tomato pieces, chopped cabbage, stock, ½ of the Liquid Smoke, crushed pepper and thyme. Simmer about 1 hour, until vegetables are done.

5. Puree and return to the pot ¾ quart of vegetables and 1 quart of the beans.

6.   Add cooked beans, their cooking liquid and remaining ½ of the Liquid Smoke, crushed pepper and thyme.

Option

Lima beans can be substituted for the white beans. Each cup of dry beans makes approximately 2½ cups cooked beans.

Serving:	1½ cups
Calories:	280
Fat grams:	1.0
% of Fat:	3%

SPLIT PEA VEGETABLE SOUP

(makes 5 quarts)

1	cup stock or water
3	cups onions, diced
3	cups celery, diced
3	large garlic cloves, diced
1	cup parsnip, diced
1	cup turnip, diced
3	cups green split peas, washed
3	quarts stock or water
¼	cup fresh parsley, finely chopped
1	tablespoon basil
1	teaspoon thyme
2	bay leaves
2	teaspoons curry powder
3	cups carrots, diced
2	cups corn, fresh or frozen
2	cups cabbage, sliced thin
2	large potatoes, peeled and cubed
2	medium zucchini, sliced
3	tablespoons light miso

1. Sauté onion, celery, garlic, parsnip and turnip in stock or water in an 8 quart stock pot.

2. Add rinsed split peas and stir, continuing to sauté until mixed well with other vegetables.

3. Add 3 quarts of stock or water and stir in parsley, basil, thyme, bay leaves and curry powder.

4. Cook for 1½ hours or until split peas are completely broken down.

5. Add carrots, corn, cabbage, potatoes and zucchini. Cook another 30 minutes or until potatoes are tender.

6. Remove 3-4 cups of soup mixture to blender; add miso and puree.

7. Return to pot and adjust flavor to taste.

'Freezer Friendly'

Serving:	1½ cups
Calories:	360
Fat grams:	1.7
% of Fat:	4%

WHITE BEAN FLORENTINE

(serves 6)

2   cups navy beans, dry
½   cup celery, chopped
½   cup carrots, chopped
½   cup onions, sliced
2   cups fresh spinach, chopped
1   tablespoon fresh oregano
1   tablespoon fresh basil
1   strip kombu
1   teaspoon garlic, minced
8   cups water
2   tablespoons tamari

1. Sort and soak beans overnight in three times the volume of water. Drain, discarding soaking water, and add 8 cups of water. Cook beans and kombu until beans are soft and creamy.

2. Add vegetables and herbs and cook 30 minutes longer.

3. Add spinach and cook 5 minutes.

4. Add tamari.

Serving:	1½ cups
Calories:	190
Fat grams:	1.0
% of Fat:	4%

Main Course
–Entrées–

7

AFRICAN SQUASH STEW

(makes 2 quarts; serves 6)

Serve over rice, potatoes or alone.

3	cups onions, diced small
2	cups stock or water
3	cups turnip, peeled, cubed
4	cups winter squash (butternut, acorn, buttercup, or delicata), peeled, cubed
8	cups cabbage (or kale or collard greens), diced, gently packed
4	tablespoons almond butter (optional)
4	tablespoons mellow barley miso
½	teaspoon turmeric
¼	teaspoon crushed red pepper (to taste)

1. Sauté onion in ¼ cup of water, briefly. Add turnip, squash and 1 cup stock or water.

2. Stir, cover and simmer over medium low heat until barely tender, about 10–15 minutes.

3. Mix together almond butter (if used), miso, turmeric and pepper in ¾ cup hot stock or water. A wire whisk is helpful.

4. Add greens and miso mixture, stir and cover to cook until greens are done, about 10 minutes, stirring occasionally.

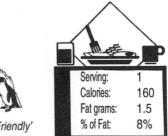

'Freezer Friendly'

Serving:	1
Calories:	160
Fat grams:	1.5
% of Fat:	8%

BLACK BEANS WITH POBLANO CHILI, CORN SAUCE

(makes 3 quarts; serves 8)

Serve over rice or baked potato.

1 lb. black beans, dry
1⅔ cups red onions, finely chopped
1⅔ tablespoons garlic, minced
5 ounces red peppers (fresh), chopped
1½ chili poblanos (also called passila) fresh, chopped (or 1 anaheim)
⅔ lb. diced tomatoes
1¼ tablespoons cider vinegar
2 teaspoons marjoram
1 teaspoon crushed dried chilies
1 bay leaf, ground
1¼ teaspoons cumin
1¼ teaspoons pasilla chili powder
Salt, to taste
Black pepper, to taste
1⅔ cups bean juice
¼ lb. frozen corn
2½ tablespoons cilantro, chopped

1. Sort beans, soak overnight. Rinse beans, discarding soaking water. Add fresh water and cook beans until done, but firm. Reserve bean juice.

2. Sauté onions; add garlic, red and poblano chilies, continue to sauté. Add seasonings, diced tomatoes, vinegar and bean juice. Simmer 15 minutes.

3. Add cooked black beans, simmer 15 minutes. Stir in corn and cilantro.

'Freezer Friendly'

Serving:	1
Calories:	230
Fat grams:	1.0
% of Fat:	3%

BAKED YAMS & APPLES

(serves 8)

6   medium yams (5 lbs.)
2   tablespoons molasses
½   cup water
4   medium red apples, peeled
½   cup orange juice
1   tablespoon orange rind, grated
1   teaspoon salt
½   cup raisins
5   large bananas, sliced
1–2 oranges, thinly sliced
     Dash of cinnamon

1. Scrub and prick yams with a fork, then bake at 425 degrees for 1 hour.

2. Meanwhile, peel, core and cut apples into ½ inch slices.

3. Heat 1 tablespoon molasses and ¼ cup water in a nonstick skillet.

4. Add apple slices and turn to coat with the mixture. Simmer very gently until barely tender, about 10 minutes, turning twice during the cooking. Reserve juice and add to yam mixture.

5. Place cooked apples on bottom of casserole or 3 quart pyrex dish. Then add sliced bananas and brush with ¼ cup of orange juice.

6. When yams are done, remove from oven, cut in half and remove pulp to a large bowl.

7. Add remaining molasses, ¼ cup orange juice, orange rind, salt and raisins. Add juice from simmering apples.

8. Mash until well mixed. Spoon yam mixture on top of the apples.

9. Spread orange slices over entire casserole. Sprinkle cinnamon over oranges.

10. Return to oven at 375 degrees for 15 minutes.

Helpful Hint

Soak raisins in the orange juice, drain before adding to yam mixture. Add soaking juice to yam mixture.

'Freezer Friendly'

Serving:	1
Calories:	390
Fat grams:	1.0
% of Fat:	2%

BAKED SAMOSAS

(makes approximately 20– 3½" diameter or 12– 5" diameter; serves 6)

Ideal for main course, finger food or hors d'oeuvres.

Filling

½	cup carrots, finely diced
½	cup frozen peas
1	teaspoon black mustard seeds
¼	cup stock
2	large cloves garlic, minced
1"	fresh ginger, peeled and grated (½ teaspoon)
1	cup onion, diced
2	large potatoes, peeled, quartered and boiled until tender
2	tablespoons mellow barley miso dissolved in 2 teaspoons water or stock
½	teaspoon coriander
1	tablespoon fresh lemon juice
	Spike or sea salt, to taste

1. Steam carrots for 5 minutes; peas for 3 minutes; set aside.

2. Heat black mustard seeds in a heavy skillet.

3. Sauté garlic, ginger and onion for 5 minutes in stock.

4. Combine with potatoes, mashing with fork until dense, but combined.

5. Add all other ingredients, except peas, and mix well.

6. Fold in peas, taking care not to smash them.

7. Taste and season with Spike or salt .

Options

Add 1 teaspoon curry powder.

Pastry

    2   cups whole wheat pastry flour
    ¾   cup finely ground almonds
    1   cup vegetable stock (cold)

1. Add flour and almonds to a food processor.

2. Add stock slowly while processing into a ball (should be sticky).

3. Roll out pastry dough on a floured board. Dough should be very thin (approximately ⅛ inch).

4. Cut into 5 inch or 2 ½ inch circles. Place a few tablespoons of filling in center of each circle, depending on the size.

5. Fold over and seal with a fork (crimp). Poke several holes in the tops.

6. Bake in preheated 350 degree oven for approximately 20 minutes or until dough is golden brown. Serve warm or cold.

Options

You may substitute 1 cup brown rice flour or spelt flour for 1 cup whole wheat pastry flour .

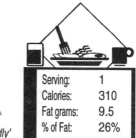

'Freezer Friendly'

Serving:	1
Calories:	310
Fat grams:	9.5
% of Fat:	26%

CARROT LOAF
(OR CRISPY BURGERS)

(makes one 2 lb. loaf; serves 6)

Top the loaf with Savory Mushroom Gravy (see Index) or any of your other favorite gravies or sauces.

1 ¾ cups grated carrots
1 ¼ cups short grained brown rice (cooked)
1 ¼ cups mashed garbanzo beans (chickpeas) (cooked)
¾ cup whole wheat bread crumbs
3 tablespoons tahini, toasted (optional).
¾ cup onion, finely chopped
¾ cup celery, finely chopped
6 tablespoons fresh parsley, finely chopped
1 clove garlic, pureed
2 teaspoons egg replacer
2 teaspoons tamari
3 tablespoons "lite" soy milk

1. Mix the carrots, rice, garbanzo beans, bread crumbs and tahini (if used), in a large bowl.

2. Sauté onions, celery, parsley and tamari in ¼ cup of water or stock in a saucepan.

3. Puree garlic clove in soy milk with egg replacer in a blender.

4. Add all ingredients, including soy milk mixture, to the carrot mixture, and mix well.

5. Press into a lightly oiled loaf pan and bake uncovered at 350 degrees for one hour.

6. When cooked, put an oblong plate on top of the loaf pan. Using pot holders, hold the two together and turn over quickly, allowing the loaf to drop out onto the plate.

Option

To make burger patties, form into 4–5 ounce balls and flatten onto a lightly oiled cookie sheet; bake for 25 minutes at 350 degrees or until golden brown. Turn over and bake 10–15 minutes more, or until crispy brown.

'Freezer Friendly'

Serving:	1
Calories:	185
Fat grams:	2.5
% of Fat:	12%

DEEP DISH ENCHILADA PIE

(serves 8)

6   cups Enchilada Sauce (See Index)
15 non-fat corn tortillas (7" diameter)
1¾ cups cooked beans (kidney, red or black)
2½ cups long grain brown rice, cooked
5¼ ounce (wt) green chilies, diced
3¼ cups zucchini, shredded, drained
1   cup onion, chopped, sautéed
6½ ounce (wt) corn
1   teaspoon salt
¼ teaspoon garlic powder
½ teaspoon chili powder
½ cup scallions, thinly sliced

1. Mix beans, rice and green chilies together with ½ cup enchilada sauce plus ½ teaspoon salt and garlic powder.

2. Mix sautéed onion, zucchini and corn together with 1 cup enchilada sauce, plus ½ teaspoon salt and chili powder.

3. Pour ½ cup enchilada sauce on bottom of a 9" X 13" pyrex pan.

4. Place 3 tortillas, lightly dipped in sauce, *but not dripping*, in sauce on bottom of pan.

5. Spread ½ bean and rice mixture over tortillas.

6. Layer 3 more tortillas, *lightly dipped* in sauce.

7. Layer ½ vegetable mixture over tortillas.

8. Layer 3 more tortillas, *lightly dipped* in sauce.

9. Repeat steps 5 through 8.

10. Cook covered in preheated 350 degree oven for 1 hour.

11. Spread light layer of sauce (approximately ½ cup) on top. Cook for 15 more minutes, uncovered. Garnish with sliced scallions.

Serving:	1
Calories:	350
Fat grams:	3.0
% of Fat:	7%

BROWN RICE CROQUETTES

(makes 6)

Serve with mushroom gravy, or your favorite sauce.

        2   cups cooked brown rice
        21   ounces "lite" tofu, firm
        1   cup onion, finely chopped
        1   cup carrot, grated
        1   cup mushrooms, finely chopped
        2   large cloves garlic, minced
        ½   cup whole wheat bread crumbs
        2   tablespoons whole wheat flour
        2   tablespoons tamari
             Freshly ground black pepper, to taste
        ½   cup water or stock for sautéing

1. Sauté garlic, onions, mushrooms and carrots until tender.

2. Mash tofu in a bowl; add cooked rice, bread crumbs and flour.

3. Mix cooked vegetables with other ingredients, adding tamari and pepper (add more flour if too loose).

4. Form croquettes (2–3 inches long). Place on a lightly oiled baking dish or cookie sheet, then bake in a preheated 375 degree oven for approximately 20 minutes or until brown.

5. Turn over and bake for 5 more minutes.

Option

To make burger patties, form into 4–5 ounce balls and flatten onto a lightly oiled cookie sheet; bake for 25 minutes at 350 degrees or until golden brown. Turn over and bake 10–15 minutes more, or until crispy brown.

'Freezer Friendly'

Serving:	1
Calories:	180
Fat grams:	2.5
% of Fat:	12%

GOLDEN POTATO STEW

(makes 3 quarts; serves 8)

½ ounce garlic, minced
¾ lb. onions, diced
¾ lb. celery, diced
¾ lb. carrots, diced
⅓ lb. red pepper, diced
½ lb. garbanzo beans (chickpeas) (dry)
1 28 ounce can tomato sauce
1 tablespoon golden vegetable broth base
4 lbs. potatoes, chunked 1"
¾ tablespoon curry powder
⅛ teaspoon cayenne
3 cups bean liquid (if needed)

1. Sort and soak beans overnight in three times as much water; drain. Cook soaked beans in three times again as much water; drain. Reserve 3 cups bean water.

2. Steam potatoes until *al dente*.

3. Sauté garlic, onions, celery, carrots and red pepper for 10 minutes.

4. Add beans, bean liquid, tomato sauce, golden broth, potatoes, curry and cayenne.

5. Simmer for 30–40 minutes, until potatoes are tender, or 1 hour in a 350 degree oven.

Serving:	1
Calories:	385
Fat grams:	2.5
% of Fat:	6%

EGGPLANT VEGETABLE RAGOUT (MEXICAN)

(makes 4 quarts; serves 10)

Serve over polenta, pasta or rice.

1	eggplant, washed, cut in 1" cubes
1	green pepper, thinly sliced
2	cups onion, chopped
6	cloves garlic, crushed
3	cups frozen corn
2	28 ounce cans tomato sauce
2	15 ounce cans stewed tomatoes
1	6 ounce can tomato paste (optional)
¼	cup green chilies, diced
4	cups cooked beans (kidney, pinto or black)
½	cup apple juice
¼	cup cumin
2	tablespoons pasilla chili powder
2	teaspoons oregano
1	tablespoon chili powder
1	tablespoon cilantro, chopped
2	tablespoons red miso
	Salt & pepper, to taste

1. Sauté onions in water; add garlic & green pepper.
2. Add tomato sauce, stewed tomatoes, seasonings, eggplant and miso.
3. Simmer for 2 hours, covered, then add diced chilies, cooked beans and frozen corn and apple juice. (Add tomato paste if not thick enough.)
4. Simmer for 5 more minutes, uncovered.
5. Add salt and pepper, to taste.

Option

Italian Version: to make this dish Italian, make the following modifications:

1. Omit cumin, pasilla chili powder, oregano, chili powder and cilantro.

2. Reduce corn to 2 cups and add 4 zucchini, cut lengthwise, then sliced, instead of cooked beans.

3. Substitute ¼ cup Italian seasoning mix, 1 teaspoon thyme and 1 teaspoon basil for cumin, chili powders, oregano and cilantro.

4. Reduce cooking time to 1 hour. Then add zucchini, corn and apple juice. Simmer 30 minutes. Add tomato paste, if needed.

5. Season with salt and pepper.

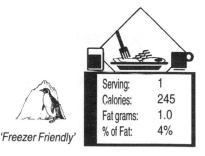

'Freezer Friendly'

Serving:	1
Calories:	245
Fat grams:	1.0
% of Fat:	4%

FIESTA CHILI

(makes 5 quarts; serves 12)

Serve over rice or baked potato, or in a burrito.

5   cups dried kidney beans, cooked*
3   onions
9   cloves garlic
1   7 ounce can whole green chilies, rinsed
2½ quarts. tomato sauce
3   tablespoons California Chili Powder
2½ tablespoons New Mexico Chili Powder
2   tablespoons chili powder
1½ tablespoons oregano, ground in mill
2   tablespoons ground cumin
1   tablespoon paprika
½   teaspoon cayenne pepper
2   bay leaves
1   tablespoon tamari
½   teaspoon sea salt
2   cups vegetable stock

1. Process onions and garlic in a food processor until very fine.

2. Sauté in ½ cup of stock for 10 minutes.

3. Remove seeds from green chilies; rinse and process in food processor until very fine.

4. Add all ingredients except tamari and salt to pot and simmer for 45 minutes or more, stirring often.

5. Add tamari and salt, stir and adjust seasonings to taste.

*Soak beans overnight in three times as much water. Drain and cover again with water and place in a large pot. Bring to a boil; cover and simmer over medium heat for one hour. Drain beans and add three times the volume of fresh water and cook for another hour. Drain beans.

Helpful Hint

The different chili powders are usually available on a special rack in supermarkets. However, if you cannot or don't have the time to find all the different kinds of chilies, add up the quantity and use any mild chili powder.

'Freezer Friendly'

Serving:	1
Calories:	180
Fat grams:	1.0
% of Fat:	4%

HOLIDAY LOAF

(serves 6)

Serve with Savory Mushroom Gravy (See Index).

1¾ cups cooked short grain brown rice
¼   cup cooked wild rice
1   cup "lite" soy milk or rice milk*
2   cups whole wheat bread crumbs
1   cup walnuts, chopped (optional)
1½ cups onion, finely chopped
1   cup celery, finely chopped
2   tablespoons chopped fresh parsley (or 1 tablespoon dried)
2   tablespoons tamari
1   teaspoon dried basil
¼   teaspoon sage
¼   teaspoon paprika
    Dash fresh black pepper
¼   teaspoon salt (optional)
3   teaspoons egg replacer

1. Add egg replacer to soy or rice milk and mix in a blender until foamy.

2. Place all ingredients in a bowl and mix well.

3. Press firmly into a lightly oiled nonstick loaf pan.

4. Bake at 350 degrees for 1 hour.

5. Slide thin, sharp knife between loaf and pan. Place serving plate on top and turn over quickly, letting loaf drop out onto plate.

Cashew milk can be used, but it makes for a richer (higher fat) loaf. To make a thick cashew milk, use ½ cup cashews blended with ¾ cup water.

Helpful Hint

Makes a great stuffing. Can also be served as Sloppy Joes covered with marinara.

Option

To make burger patties, form into 4–5 ounce balls and flatten onto a lightly oiled cookie sheet; bake for 25 minutes at 350 degrees or until golden brown. Turn over and bake 10–15 minutes more, or until crispy brown.

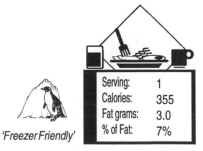

'Freezer Friendly'

Serving:	1
Calories:	355
Fat grams:	3.0
% of Fat:	7%

BASIC POLENTA

(makes 2 quarts; serves 6)

6   cups water
1   cup polenta
1   cup medium cornmeal
2   teaspoons salt
⅔   cup onions, diced
⅔   cup frozen corn

For Italiano, add

¼   cup roasted red pepper, diced
½   cup scallions, sliced
1   teaspoon garlic powder

1. Bring water to a boil, add salt and turn off flame.

2. Pour in polenta and whisk briskly.

3. Whisk thoroughly every minute for 10 minutes or until polenta thickens.

4. Pour into casserole dish, lasagna pan or muffin pans, cover and bake at 325 degrees until set.

5. Let cool 10 minutes covered, then uncover.

Serving:	1
Calories:	170
Fat grams:	1.5
% of Fat:	8%

LAYERED PASTA CASSEROLE

(serves 8)

1   lb. linguini
1¾ lb. "lite" tofu, firm
2   quarts tomato sauce, Basic Marinara or Bolognese (See Index)
1   tablespoon nutritional yeast
1   teaspoon onion powder
1   tablespoon + 1 teaspoon garlic, minced
1½ teaspoons salt
⅓   cup parsley, finely chopped
1½ tablespoons basil

1. Cook linguini until *al dente*.
2. Toss pasta with ¾ of the tomato sauce.
3. Mix other ingredients with tofu in a food processor until the consistency of ricotta (smooth and creamy).
4. Layer in a pan* :

      1½ " linguini
      ¾ " tofu ricotta
      1½ " linguini

5. Heat in 350 degree oven, covered (if using foil, place parchment paper on top, then foil) for 30–40 minutes, depending on the density of the casserole.

Use a lasagna pan, baking dish or crock type serving dish.

Serving:	1
Calories:	255
Fat grams:	2.8
% of Fat:	8%

LENTIL STEW

(makes 4 quarts; serves 10)

Serve over rice or baked potato.

1   large onion, chopped
2   cloves garlic, chopped
2   stalks celery, sliced
2   tablespoons dark miso (traditional or red)
1   15 ounce can tomato pieces, drained
2   carrots, diced
6–7 cups water or vegetable stock
1   teaspoon oregano
1   teaspoon basil
½   teaspoon thyme
½   teaspoon marjoram
3   cups dry lentils, rinsed
1   medium yam, peeled and diced
¼   cup fresh parsley, chopped
2   large tomatoes, chopped (optional)

1. Sauté onions, garlic, celery, and carrots in ½ cup stock or water for 3–5 minutes.

2. Add miso and stir to dissolve; then add tomato pieces. Add herbs and sauté one additional minute.

3. Add remaining stock or water, lentils, yam, and parsley.

4. Cook uncovered until lentils are tender, about 1 hour. Stir occasionally, checking water level. Add water as necessary as lentils swell.

Options

Substitute green onions or leeks for onion.

Substitute Italian seasoning for herbs.

'Freezer Friendly'

Serving:	1
Calories:	180
Fat grams:	1.0
% of Fat:	4%

LIGHT LENTIL LOAF

(makes one 2 lb. loaf; serves 6)

Serve with Savory Mushroom Gravy or Country Style Gravy (See Index).

1¼ cups cooked short grained brown rice
1¼ cups cooked lentils, mashed
1½ cups onions, chopped
1¼ cups carrots, grated
3   cloves garlic, diced
3   tablespoons stock or water
1¼ cups raw oats
4   teaspoons dark miso (traditional or red)
2   teaspoons tamari
4   teaspoons hot stock or water
5   tablespoons fresh parsley, finely chopped
2   teaspoons sage
¾   teaspoon celery seed

1. Sauté onions, carrots and garlic in stock or water.

2. Mix with cooked rice, lentils and oats.

3. Mix miso and tamari with hot stock or water to dissolve. Add to mixture.

4. Add parsley, sage and celery seed. Mix until all ingredients are combined.

5. Pack into lightly oiled loaf pan and bake at 350 degrees for 1 hour. Slide a thin, sharp knife between the loaf and the pan. Place serving plate on top and turn over quickly, letting loaf drop out onto plate.

Option

To make burger patties, form into 4–5 ounce balls and flatten onto a lightly oiled cookie sheet; bake for 25 minutes at 350 degrees or until golden brown. Turn over and bake 10–15 minutes more, or until crispy brown.

'Freezer Friendly'

Serving:	1
Calories:	190
Fat grams:	2.0
% of Fat:	8%

MACARONI AND "CHEEZE"

(makes 2½ quarts; serves 6)

1	lb. dry macaroni noodles
2	cups water
1	cup raw cashews
2	tablespoons nutritional yeast
1	teaspoon salt
1	teaspoon garlic powder
1	tablespoon onion powder (or 1 cup chopped onion)
4	ounces roasted red pepper (for color)
2	tablespoons lemon juice
½	cup whole wheat bread crumbs

1. Cook macaroni noodles in water and drain. Set aside.

2. Process cashews to a fine meal consistency. Add water, a small amount at a time, and process until smooth.

3. Add nutritional yeast, red pepper, garlic powder, onion powder and lemon juice, and blend until mixed.

4. Combine cashew milk mixture and cooked macaroni in a pyrex baking dish.

5. Bake covered at 350 degrees for 20 minutes. Uncover and top with bread crumbs; bake 10 more minutes until bread crumbs are brown.

Options

Add 1 cup fresh or frozen peas with cooked noodles.

Add fresh sliced tomatoes on top, before bread crumbs.

Serving:	1
Calories:	395
Fat grams:	12.0
% of Fat:	27%

MUNG BEAN POTATO CASSEROLE

(makes 3 quarts; serves 8)

2 cups dry mung beans
2 large cloves garlic, minced
1¼ cups onions, diced
2 tablespoons vegetarian chicken-style broth powder
4 cups water, heated
2¼ lbs. potatoes, peeled, chunked and steamed
1 cup celery, diced (optional)
1 cup carrots, diced
½ teaspoon salt
¼ teaspoon white pepper
⅛ teaspoon crushed red pepper

1. Sort and soak mung beans overnight in three times their volume of water. Drain, discarding soaking water, and rinse.

2. Dissolve chicken-style broth powder in heated water to make stock.

3. Sauté garlic and onions in a little water or stock in a large skillet.

4. Add mung beans, celery (if used), carrots, and chicken-style broth, simmer, uncovered, for ½ hour. Stir occasionally.

5. Add cooked potatoes, salt, white pepper and crushed pepper, and simmer for another 2–3 minutes.

Serving:	1
Calories:	235
Fat grams:	1.0
% of Fat:	2%

MUSHROOM STROGANOFF

(serves 6)

Serve over hot pasta or rice.

¼ cup stock or water
6 cloves garlic, minced
½ cup onion, finely minced
2 lbs. mushrooms, sliced
6 tablespoons brandy (option: marsala wine or apple
   juice)
¼ cup tamari
2 tablespoons worcestershire sauce (without
   anchovies)
2 cups cashew milk*
2 tablespoons arrowroot
1 lb. cooked fetuccini

1. Sauté garlic and onion in stock or water until translucent.

2. Add mushrooms and continue to sauté for 10 minutes.

3. Add brandy (or wine, or juice), tamari and worcestershire sauce and cook another 5 minutes.

4. Stir in cashew milk and arrowroot mixture and simmer until thickened, about 5 minutes.

Mix 3/4 cup cashews and enough water to make 2 cups. Blend until creamy, add arrowroot and blend until smooth.

Serving:	1
Calories:	300
Fat grams:	9.0
% of Fat:	26%

OVEN BAKED BEANS

(makes 5 quarts; serves 16)

5¼ quarts cooked kidney beans
½ lb. onion, diced
2   quarts tomato juice
1   cup barbecue sauce
1   cup molasses
1   cup apple juice concentrate
1   cup orange juice concentrate
¼   cup worcestershire sauce (without anchovies)
1   tablespoon salt, to taste
1   tablespoon curry powder
1   tablespoon dry mustard
1   tablespoon vinegar
1½ teaspoons Liquid Smoke

1. Sort and soak beans overnight in three times their volume of water. Discard soaking water. Cook beans, using water equal to three times their volume, to final desired doneness; drain. Use cooking liquid for other uses, if needed.

2. Combine cooked beans, onions, tomato juice, barbecue sauce, molasses, apple and orange juice concentrate, curry, dry mustard, vinegar and Liquid Smoke. Add worcestershire sauce and salt.

3. Bake covered, at 300 degrees for 1 hour and at 250 degrees for 5 hours. (A large crockpot is great for this!)

Option

To make into "Franks & Beans," add 1 package of Smart Dogs, cut into ½" slices, during the last half hour of baking.

'Freezer Friendly'

Serving:	1
Calories:	450
Fat grams:	1.5
% of Fat:	3%

PEPERONATA

(makes 2 quarts, serves 6)

Serve over pasta, rice or baked potato.

4   cups onions, french cut
4–5 cloves garlic, sliced
¼   teaspoon crushed hot pepper
4   bay leaves
2   cups vegetable stock or water
6   yellow, red, and green peppers, cut into strips
2   tablespoons red miso
4   tomatoes, peeled and chopped, or 1 28 ounce can,
      chopped
1   tablespoon arrowroot dissolved in ¼ cup tomato juice
      or water
      Freshly ground black pepper, to taste

1. Sauté onions, garlic, and crushed pepper in ½ cup stock for 5 minutes.

2. Add pepper strips, bay leaves, and ½ cup more stock, and cook for 5 minutes over medium flame, stirring often.

3. Dissolve miso in ½ cup hot stock.

4. Add mixture plus chopped tomatoes and remaining stock and cook 5–7 minutes longer or until peppers are tender.

5. Push peppers aside and add dissolved arrowroot mixture to liquid; stir to thicken.

6. Add black pepper to taste.

'Freezer Friendly'

Serving:	1
Calories:	110
Fat grams:	1.0
% of Fat:	6%

RATATOUILLE

(serves 4)

Serve over pasta, polenta, rice or any other hot grain.

1	lb. small or medium zucchini, cut into ½" cubes
1	small eggplant, cut into ½" cubes
1	onion, french cut, and halved
¼	cup tomato juice, fresh or canned
4	cloves garlic, minced
1	28 ounce can tomato pieces, drained
1	cup green pepper, chunked (½ green and ½ red adds color)
1	teaspoon oregano
1	teaspoon basil
	Tamari, to taste
	Sea salt, to taste
	Freshly ground black pepper, to taste

1. Sauté eggplant, onion and garlic in ¼ cup of tomato juice in a large skillet.

2. Cook for 5 minutes or until eggplant just softens.

3. Stir in tomato pieces, green peppers, zucchini and all the herbs.

4. Cook covered over medium heat 10–15 minutes. *Be careful not to burn!*

Ratatouille Sauce

1	cup tomato sauce
1	tablespoon frozen apple juice concentrate
1	tablespoon arrowroot
1	tablespoon lemon juice, fresh squeezed

1. Combine all ingredients and cook until sauce thickens, about 15 minutes.

2. Pour over vegetables and cook until vegetables are tender, but not mushy.

3. Season to taste.

'Freezer Friendly'

Serving:	1
Calories:	90
Fat grams:	1.0
% of Fat:	7%

ROASTED HERBED POTATOES & VEGETABLES

(6 quarts)

Serve hot as a main entrée or side dish.

1   lb. green and red peppers, cut in medium-size pieces
2   lbs. zucchini or other squash, ½" sliced
2   lbs. medium mushrooms, whole if small, halved if large
2   lbs. red onion, chunks
6   lbs. red potatoes, cut in large eighths
2   lbs. asparagus, trimmed, cut in ½ (seasonal)
1¾ cups frozen corn
    Salt, to taste
    Freshly ground black pepper, to taste
½   bunch fresh thyme or rosemary (or dried herbs)

1. Boil potatoes until *al dente*, 3–4 minutes.

2. Blanch asparagus for 20 seconds, if used.

3. Toss all vegetables together plus herbs, salt and pepper.

4. Lay in pans *in one layer* and cook in *hot* oven, 550 degrees for 15 minutes.

Serving:	1½ cups
Calories:	210
Fat grams:	1.0
% of Fat:	3%

SCALLOPED POTATOES

(serves 6)

1   quart potatoes, unpeeled, thinly sliced
2½ cups soy milk (or nut milk*--optional)
1   teaspoon sea salt
1   teaspoon onion powder, flakes or ¼ cup onion,
    chopped
    Paprika

1. Place potatoes in a lightly oiled baking dish.

2. Liquefy all other ingredients and pour over potatoes.

3. Cover with parchment paper, then foil, and bake for 1 to 1½ hours at 375 degrees.

4. Test for doneness.

5. Remove foil and parchment paper, sprinkle with paprika and return to oven just long enough to brown.

*To make nut milk, pour 2 cups of water into a blender. Blend on low while adding ½ heaping cup of cashew nuts; continue at low speed for 30 seconds. Blend on high for 2½ minutes until creamy. This makes for a richer dish, but is an alternative for those who are looking to eliminate soy products.

Serving:	1
Calories:	95
Fat grams:	1.0
% of Fat:	8%

SHEPHERD'S PIE

(serves 6)

Serve with Savory Mushroom Gravy or Country Style Gravy (See Index).

2   cups onions, diced
2   cups frozen corn
2   cups frozen peas
2   cups carrots, diced and blanched
1⅓ cups soy milk (or nut milk*--optional)
2   cloves garlic, minced
2   tablespoons fresh basil or 1 tablespoon dried
½   teaspoon thyme
½   teaspoon marjoram
2   lbs. potatoes, peeled (store in water to avoid turning black)

1. Sauté onions with herbs and garlic for 10 minutes.
2. Add carrots; cook until soft. Add corn and peas.
3. Pour ⅔ cup milk over vegetables and braise for 10 minutes.
4. While vegetables are baking, steam and mash potatoes with reserved ⅔ cup milk. (This can be done in advance.)
5. Mix thoroughly and arrange by spoonfuls on top of vegetables until completely covered.
6. Turn oven to broil and brown potatoes until golden brown.

To make nut milk, pour 1 cup of water into a blender. Blend on low while adding ⅓ heaping cup of cashew nuts; continue at low speed for 30 seconds. Blend on high for 2 ½ minutes until creamy. This makes for a richer dish, but is an alternative for those who are looking to eliminate soy products.

Option

Sprinkle with paprika.

Serving:	1
Calories:	270
Fat grams:	1.5
% of Fat:	5%

SLOPPY JOES

(makes 1 quart)

Serve over whole wheat rolls or rice.

1	cup dry lentils
3	cups water
8	ounces tomato sauce
2	tablespoons barbecue sauce
2	tablespoons ketchup
½	cup green pepper, finely chopped
½	cup onion, finely chopped
2	tablespoons stock or water
1	teaspoon garlic granules
1	teaspoon paprika
1	tablespoon A-1 sauce
1	teaspoon tamari
3	tablespoons orange juice
½	teaspoon sea salt

1. Cook lentils in water until tender, about 45 minutes. Drain lentils, leaving a little water in the pot.

2. Sauté green pepper and onion in stock or water until tender.

3. Add all remaining ingredients to pot of lentils and simmer covered, 30–45 minutes until flavors have blended.

'Freezer Friendly'

Serving:	1 cup
Calories:	210
Fat grams:	1.0
% of Fat:	3%

SPICY YAM STEW

(makes 2½ quarts; serves 6)

Serve over grain, pasta or alone.

- ½ cups stock or water
- 2   medium yams, peeled and cubed
- 2   cups celery, thickly sliced on diagonal
- 1   green pepper, roughly chopped
- 1   large onion, french cut
- 2   cups carrots, quartered and cut in 1-inch chunks
- 1   16 ounce can whole tomatoes, cut in pieces, with juice
- 3" piece of stick cinnamon
     Tamari, to taste
     Freshly ground black pepper, to taste
     Pinch of cayenne, to taste *(careful!)*
- 2   tablespoons arrowroot dissolved in 2 tablespoons water
- ¼   cup freshly chopped parsley, as garnish

1. Place all ingredients except arrowroot and garnish in a large soup pot and simmer for 30 minutes, stirring occasionally, or until all the vegetables are tender. (This stew can also be cooked, covered, in the oven, stirring often.)

2. Add dissolved arrowroot, stir until slightly thickened, and adjust seasonings to taste. Garnish.

Helpful Hint

This is a "chunky" stew, so make sure the vegetables are prepared and sliced in 1 inch pieces.

'Freezer Friendly'

Serving:	1
Calories:	175
Fat grams:	1.0
% of Fat:	3%

STUFFED MANICOTTI

(serves 4)

8   manicotti noodle shells (jumbo)
¾   lb. "lite" tofu, firm
½   teaspoon oregano
½   teaspoon thyme
1   teaspoon fresh basil, minced (or ½ teaspoon dried)
2   teaspoons garlic, minced
⅓   cup fresh parsley, minced (or 1 tablespoon dried)
¼   teaspoon white pepper
    Sea salt, to taste
3   cups Basic Marinara or Bolognese Sauce (See Index)
    Fresh parsley or basil, for garnish

1. Preheat oven to 375 degrees.
2. Bring large pot of water to a boil. Add pasta shells and bring to a boil again. Cook pasta for 5–6 minutes in boiling water, rinse in cold water, and set aside, making sure the shells are not stacked or overlapping.
3. Mix all filling ingredients except marinara sauce in a large bowl or food processor.
4. Stuff shells with filling and place into a lightly oiled or nonstick baking dish (pyrex is fine).
5. Pour marinara sauce over stuffed shells and bake, uncovered, for 30 minutes, or until sauce is bubbling. Garnish with fresh herbs and serve.

Helpful Hint

This recipe can be made ahead, kept in the refrigerator or frozen until ready to bake.

Serving:	1
Calories:	140
Fat grams:	1.5
% of Fat:	10%

SPICY VEGETABLE STEW

(makes 4 quarts; serves 10)

Serve over rice

½ cup vegetable stock (or water)
2 cups sliced onion (french cut)
4–6 garlic cloves, crushed
3 stalks celery, sliced (12 ounces)
30 boiling or pearl onions (or 2 onions, chunked)
3 potatoes, chunked
3 carrots, sliced (12 ounce)
2 zucchini, chunked (16 ounce)
1 green pepper, chunked (6 ounce)
¾ lb. string beans, sliced
3 broccoli stalks, sliced
1 lb. large mushrooms, quartered
1 15 ounce can tomato pieces, (reserve juice for arrowroot)
1 cup tomato sauce
½ cup apple juice
4 dried tomatoes, finely chopped (after soaking in hot water)
3 tablespoons tamari
2 teaspoons hot oriental dry mustard
3 tablespoons parsley flakes
3 teaspoons chili powder
2 teaspoons thyme
2 teaspoons basil
1 teaspoon oregano
1 teaspoon cumin
   Tabasco, to taste
3 tablespoons arrowroot

1. Take all dried spices and grind in a coffee grinder, or mortar and pestle, or Japanese suribachi.

2. Put all vegetables and other ingredients except arrowroot into a large heavy pot, stirring to mix well.

3. Cover and remove to 350 degree oven for about 2½ hours or to desired tenderness, mixing and basting every 20 minutes for a braised quality.

4. Just before serving, mix 3 tablespoons arrowroot with ¼ cup tomato juice and stir into stew until thickened (if needed).

Helpful Hint

This is a "chunky" stew, so make sure the vegetables are prepared and sliced in 1 inch pieces.

Be careful not to use too much tabasco. *Remember,* you can always add, but you cannot take away.

'Freezer Friendly'

Serving:	1
Calories:	140
Fat grams:	1.0
% of Fat:	6%

SPRING BARLEY LOAF

(serves 6)

Serve with Savory Mushroom Gravy or Country Style Gravy (See Index).

    2   cups cooked barley*
    2   cups whole wheat bread crumbs
    1   cup scallions, chopped
    ½   cup raw, unpeeled potato, grated
    ¼   cup green pepper, minced
    ½   cup zucchini, grated
    ½   cup "lite" soy milk
    1   large clove garlic
    1   tablespoon egg replacer
    2   tablespoons low sodium tamari
    1   tablespoon tahini, toasted (optional)
    1   tablespoon mellow light miso
    1½   teaspoons marjoram
         Dash freshly ground black pepper
         Pinch sea salt, to taste

1. Wash and drain 1 cup dry barley. Cook in 2 cups boiling water for 45 minutes or until tender.

2. Mix together cooked barley, bread crumbs, scallions, potato, green pepper, and zucchini.

3. Blend soy milk, garlic and egg replacer on high speed until foamy, 2–3 minutes. Add to loaf mixture.

4. Combine tamari, tahini and miso and add to the loaf mixture. Add marjoram, pepper and salt, if desired, and knead well with hands.

5. Pack into lightly oiled loaf pan and bake at 350 degrees for 1¼ hours.

Preferably unhulled, but if not available, use pearl. If using unhulled, cover loaf with parchment paper to prevent from getting burned and hard.

Option

To make burger patties, form into 4–5 ounce balls and flatten onto a lightly oiled cookie sheet; bake for 25 minutes at 350 degrees or until golden brown. Turn over and bake 10–15 minutes more, or until crispy brown.

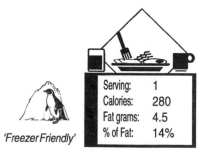

'Freezer Friendly'

Serving:	1
Calories:	280
Fat grams:	4.5
% of Fat:	14%

STUFFED CABBAGE ROLLS

(serves 8)

2   heads cabbage
1   onion, finely chopped
½   lb. mushrooms, finely chopped
¾   cup currants or raisins
½   cup water or stock
½   teaspoon nutmeg
¼   teaspoon garlic powder
    Dash freshly ground black pepper
3   cups cooked brown rice (short grain)
2   quarts tomato sauce or Basic Marinara Sauce (See Index)

1. Remove core from cabbages.

2. Steam or immerse cabbage in boiling water 5–10 minutes, peeling off leaves carefully and setting aside as they become cooked. (Save center core of leaves which are too small for rolls, chop up and add to marinara or tomato sauce, while simmering).

3. Sauté onions, mushrooms and currants or raisins in ½ cup water or stock for 10 minutes. Stir in nutmeg, garlic powder and pepper.

4. Stir in brown rice and 1 cup of the tomato sauce. Remove from heat.

5. Pour 1 cup tomato sauce over the bottom of a 9" x 12" baking dish.

6. Cut out tough center piece of each cabbage leaf. Spoon about ⅓–½ cup rice mixture into center of each cabbage leaf. Roll up and place seam side down in baking dish. Leave enough room between rolls so they are not touching.

7. Pour remaining tomato sauce over the rolls in the baking dish.

8. Cover with parchment paper and aluminum foil and bake at 400 degrees for 15 minutes, then reduce to 350 degrees and bake for one hour and 15 minutes (the longer it cooks, the more tender the cabbage rolls get).

Option

You may add currants (or raisins) to the marinara sauce, for a sweeter taste. A dash of lemon gives a sweet and sour flavor.

Helpful Hint

May be prepared ahead. Keeps well in the refrigerator. Bake just before serving and add 15 minutes of baking time.

'Freezer Friendly'

Serving:	1
Calories:	240
Fat grams:	2.0
% of Fat:	6%

TAMALE LOAF

(makes 2 quarts / serves 6)

2   cups corn
2½ cups tomato pieces, with juice
½   lb. onions, chopped
½   tablespoon salt
½   teaspoon garlic
2½ ounces (wt) potato starch
1   cup "lite" soy milk
1   cup water
¾   teaspoon cumin
¾   teaspoon paprika
1   cup polenta
2   ounces canned diced green chilies (optional)

1. Cook corn, tomato pieces, onions, salt and garlic (and chilies, if used) for 15–20 minutes on stove top in heavy skillet.

2. Mix potato starch, soy milk, water, cumin, paprika and polenta together and mix well with whisk to insure there are no lumps in polenta.

3. Mix all ingredients together while first mixture is still *hot*.

4. Pour into crock or pyrex dish.

5. Bake at 350 degrees for 1 hour, uncovered.

6. For best results, allow mixture to set up. Reheat before serving.

'Freezer Friendly'

Serving:	1
Calories:	170
Fat grams:	2.5
% of Fat:	12%

VEGETABLE STUFFED POTATOES

(serves 8)

Serve topped with Savory Mushroom or Country Style Gravy (See Index).

4   medium potatoes, baked
½   cup "lite" soy milk
¼   teaspoon onion powder
¼   teaspoon garlic powder
⅛   teaspoon freshly ground black pepper
10 ounces blanched vegetables
2   cups of gravy

1. Bake potatoes at 450 degrees until soft, about 60 minutes (depending upon the size of the potatoes).

2. While potatoes are still hot, cut in half and, using a potholder to hold each potato, gently scrape pulp from skin, taking care not to tear skin. (This process should allow the potato skin to remain firm, if not crisp.)

3. Place potato insides, soy milk, onion powder, garlic powder and pepper in a large bowl.

4. Mash with potato masher or blend until smooth.

5. Stir in cooked vegetables.

6. Divide mixture among the potato skins and top with a small amount of gravy.

7. Place stuffed potatoes on a nonstick baking sheet. Bake at 400 degrees until lightly browned, about 15 minutes.

Serving:	1
Calories:	150
Fat grams:	1.0
% of Fat:	5%

VEGETABLE LASAGNA

(makes 1 hotel pan - 15 lbs; serves 16)

3   lbs. tofu "ricotta" (See below)
3   quarts Basic Marinara Sauce (See Index)
1   quart water
4   lbs. one of these: shredded zucchini, carrot, sliced
      mushrooms or chopped spinach
1¾ lbs. lasagna noodles (15 pieces)

"Ricotta"

3   lbs. "lite" tofu, firm
1½ tablespoons nutritional yeast
1½ teaspoons onion powder
2   tablespoons garlic, minced
2½ teaspoons salt
¾   cup parsley, finely chopped
2½ tablespoons basil

1. Mix all "ricotta" ingredients with tofu until the consistency of ricotta (smooth and creamy).

2. Mix water and marinara. Layer in hotel pan or two regular lasagna pans (freeze one). Layering procedure:

      5 cups marinara and water mixture
      5 lasagna noodles
      1½ lbs. "ricotta" filling
      2 lbs. vegetables
      5 lasagna noodles
      5 cups marinara and water mixture
      1½ lbs. "ricotta" filling
      2 lbs. vegetables
      5 lasagna noodles
      5 cups marinara and water mixture

3. Cover with parchment paper, then aluminum foil, seal tightly. Cook at 375 degrees for one hour. Check to see if noodles are tender.

4. Cook 15 minutes more, if needed. Leave covered for 10 minutes after cooking.

Serving:	1
Calories:	355
Fat grams:	4.0
% of Fat:	10%

YAM & POTATO CASSEROLE

(serves 4)

8   russet potatoes, sliced (⅛" thick)
2   medium yams, peeled, sliced
1   onion, french cut
½   teaspoon crushed red pepper
¼   stock or water
     Spike, to taste

1. Pour stock or water in a large casserole dish.

2. Line bottom with approximately ⅓ of the onion slices, then potatoes, then yams.

3. Sprinkle crushed red pepper on potatoes.

4. Repeat layering until all vegetables are used.

5. Sprinkle half of the layers with Spike, to taste.

6. Cover and bake at 350 degrees for 45 minutes.

7. Check to see if stock or water has dried up. If so, add ⅛ cup more liquid, basting occasionally from bottom of casserole.

8. Return covered for 30 more minutes until potatoes are tender.

Serving:	1
Calories:	365
Fat grams:	0
% of Fat:	1%

VEGETABLE POT PIE

(makes 2 quarts; serves 6)

Sauce
- 2   cups stock or water
- ½   cup cashew pieces
- ¼   cup sesame seeds
- 2½   tablespoons vegetarian chicken-style broth powder
- 2   tablespoons potato starch
- ½   teaspoon sea salt

1. Blend all sauce ingredients in a blender or food processor.

Vegetables
- ½   cup onion, diced
- 1   cup mushrooms, sliced
- ½   cup celery, diced
- 2   cups carrots, diced
- 2   cups potatoes, peeled, diced
- 2   cups frozen peas
- 1   red pepper or pimento, diced

1. Sauté onions and mushrooms in stock or water.

2. Steam carrots, celery and potatoes separately, *al dente.*

3. Combine sauce, onions, mushrooms, celery, carrots, potatoes, peas and pimentos. Stir well.

Biscuit Topping
- 2   cups whole wheat pastry flour
- 1   teaspoon (rounded) baking powder
- ½   teaspoon baking soda
- 1   teaspoon Sucanat
- ½   teaspoon salt
- 1   teaspoon dill
- 1¼   cup soy milk or rice milk

1. Keep vegetables warm while preparing biscuit topping. Work quickly so vegetables do not overcook.

2. Place dry ingredients for topping in a bowl. Add liquid and fold in gently but thoroughly.

3. Place warm vegetables and sauce into a casserole baking dish and cover with biscuit topping by dropping spoonfuls on top of the vegetables.

4. Bake uncovered for 20–25 minutes at 400 degrees.

'Freezer Friendly'

Serving:	1
Calories:	380
Fat grams:	11.0
% of Fat:	24%

Desserts

8

APRICOT GINGER PIE

(serves 8)

¼ cup cold water
1½ packages Ginger Snaps
3 cups apple juice
½ lb. dried apricots (organic, unsulphured)
3 tablespoons agar agar flakes
1–2 tablespoons brown rice syrup, to taste
1 lb. "lite" tofu, extra firm

Crust

1. Blend ginger snaps with about ¼ cup cold water to a paste in a food processor. Press into pie pan bottom and up the sides (no need to oil).

2. Bake at 350 degrees for maximum 15–20 minutes. Let cool. If crust rises considerably, take a large spoon and press crust into pan.

Filling

1. Pour apple juice into a pot and add apricots, stirring constantly while bringing to a simmer.

2. Add agar agar flakes and continue simmering for 40 minutes.* Add rice syrup, stir again and let cool.

3. Blend tofu thoroughly in a food processor. Add apricot mixture. Bring to a creamy consistency, about 3–4 minutes. Spoon mixture with a rubber spatula into pie crust and refrigerate 1–2 hours.

4. For firmer pie, refrigerate longer. Top can be decorated with orange zest and mint leaves.

For quicker cooking, soak the apricots overnight in apple juice. Reduce simmering time to 20 minutes.

Serving:	1
Calories:	290
Fat grams:	4.5
% of Fat:	15%

BAKED BANANAS

(serves 6)

4   tablespoons apple juice
⅓   cup Sucanat
¼   teaspoon ground cloves
2   tablespoons orange juice
     Rind of ½ orange
1   teaspoon lemon juice
1"   piece of fresh ginger, peeled and grated
4   teaspoons arrowroot
6   bananas (not over ripe), sliced in half lengthwise

1. Preheat oven to 375 degrees.

2. Blend apple juice and Sucanat together until pale and soft.

3. Add cloves, orange juice, lemon juice, ginger and arrowroot. Blend until well mixed.

4. Lay bananas on a well sprayed medium baking dish and spread mixture over them.

5. Put dish in oven and bake for 10–15 minutes or until top is bubbling and bananas are cooked through and tender. Serve hot.

Serving:	1
Calories:	130
Fat grams:	1.0
% of Fat:	7%

CARROT CAKE

(serves 12)

2½ cups whole wheat pastry flour or spelt flour
2   teaspoons cinnamon
½   teaspoon nutmeg
½   teaspoon cloves
½   teaspoon allspice
1½ teaspoons baking soda
2   teaspoons baking powder
¾   cup honey
1   cup applesauce
4   teaspoons egg replacer
4   tablespoons pineapple juice
3   cups grated carrots
8   ounces* crushed pineapple, well drained (save 4
     tablespoons juice for egg replacer)
¾   cup raisins
1   cup chopped walnuts or almonds (optional)

1. Mix and sift flour, spices, baking soda, and powder.

2. Combine applesauce, honey, egg replacer and pineapple juice in blender; whiz until foamy.

3. Add carrots, pineapple, raisins, nuts (if used) and applesauce mixture to dry ingredients. Mix well.

4. Turn into a 13" x 9" x 2" nonstick baking pan (or two 8" round cake pans). Bake at 350 degrees for 1 hour.

5. Remove to cooling rack and let cool before frosting or slicing.

* It takes two 15 ounce cans of crushed pineapple to net 8 ounces. Drain well, or the cake will be too moist.

Helpful Hint

Even if you have a nonstick baking dish or cake pans, you will have to lightly oil and flour your pan; otherwise it will probably stick.

Serving:	1
Calories:	210
Fat grams:	1.0
% of Fat:	3%

Option

This recipe can be used to make muffins; however, the baking time should be reduced, depending on the size of the muffins, to 35–45 minutes.

"Cream" Frosting

    2   cups pitted dates
    1   cup water (for soaking dates)
    1   cup walnuts
    2   teaspoons vanilla

1. Soak dates in water for 2 hours to soften; drain and reserve soak water.

2. Put drained dates, walnuts and vanilla in a food processor and blend gradually, adding back soak water, if needed, until creamy.

3. Frosting is best when allowed to set for 6 hours before use. Frost as you normally would.

Serving:	1
Calories:	150
Fat grams:	6.5
% of Fat:	38%

FROSTED CAROB BROWNIES

(makes ½ sheet pan; serves 12)

Dry

3   cups spelt flour
2⅔ cups + 2 tablespoons Sucanat
3   tablespoons baking powder (non-aluminum)
1   tablespoon salt

Wet

2   cups water
1   cup applesauce
½ cup carob powder
4   tablespoons egg replacer
3   tablespoons Roma or Cafix coffee substitute
4   teaspoons vanilla
1   tablespoon + ½ teaspoon lemon juice

1. Take ½ sheet pan , oil spray, lay parchment paper (if aluminum), spray again.

2. Preheat oven to 350 degrees.

3. Combine and sift dry ingredients (Sucanat will not completely break down).

4. Place wet ingredients in a blender and whiz for ½ minute.

5. Add blended wet mixture to dry ingredients in a large bowl, and beat with a spoon until smooth. Make sure to remove any lumps.

6. Spread evenly onto parchment paper covered sheet pan and bake for 25 minutes.

7. Cool on sheet.

8. After cake has cooled, spread Carob Icing evenly onto cake.

9. Score into 3" x 3" pieces.

Carob Icing   *(makes approximately 4 cups)*

½–2 cups apple juice
1   cup maple syrup
3   cups carob powder
1   cup tahini, toasted; drain oil off top

1. Place all ingredients except apple juice in a food processor.

2. Process while adding apple juice slowly through top funnel. Continue processing, stopping to scrape down with spatula, until smooth.

Serving:	1
Calories:	420
Fat grams:	9.0
% of Fat:	18%

FRUIT TOPPINGS

Serve as toppings for "Cheeze" Cake, Crepes, Waffles, Pancakes, frozen nondairy desserts or any of the Biscuits.

Raspberry Topping

(makes 2½ cups)

2½ cups fresh or frozen whole ripe raspberries
¾   cup frozen apple juice concentrate, thawed
⅓   cup frozen apple-raspberry juice concentrate,
     thawed
2½ tablespoons arrowroot

Blueberry Topping

(makes 1½ cups)

2½ cups fresh or frozen whole ripe blueberries
⅓   cup + ½ tablespoon frozen apple juice concentrate,
     thawed
     Pinch of sea salt
2   tablespoons frozen unsweetened grape juice
     concentrate, thawed
2½ tablespoons arrowroot
1   teaspoon vanilla, added after cooking

Serving:	1
Calories:	60/25
Fat grams:	0
% of Fat:	0%

Quick and Easy
Ready in 15 Minutes

'Freezer Friendly'

Cherry Topping

(makes 2½ cups)

2½ cups whole pitted fresh or frozen sweet cherries
¾   cup frozen apple juice concentrate, thawed
⅓   cup frozen mountain cherry juice concentrate,
     thawed
     Pinch of salt
2½ tablespoons arrowroot
2   drops almond flavor extract

1. Combine juices, salt (if used) and arrowroot in a small sauce pan. Heat over medium heat, stirring constantly with a whisk, to thicken.

2. Add cherries, or blueberries, or raspberries and simmer for ½ minute, stirring constantly, mixing fruit and sauce.

3. Let cool.

Quick and Easy
Ready in 15 Minutes

'Freezer Friendly'

Serving:	1
Calories:	100
Fat grams:	0
% of Fat:	0%

GERMAN CAROB CAKE

(yield one 3 layer 9" cake; serves 12)

3 ¼ cups whole wheat pastry flour or spelt flour
¾ cup toasted carob powder
1 tablespoon baking soda
¾ teaspoon salt
1 ½ cups + 3 tablespoons water
1 ½ cups + 3 tablespoons maple syrup
¾ cup apple sauce
2 ¼ teaspoons vanilla
2 $\frac{1}{4}$ tablespoons apple cider vinegar
Carob Cake Frosting (See next page)

1. Sift dry ingredients.
2. Mix wet ingredients.
3. Add dry to wet and mix thoroughly.
4. Pour into three 9–inch lightly oiled and dusted cake pans.
5. Bake at 350 degrees for 20 minutes. Remove from oven and place on cooling cake rack.
6. Let cool before frosting.

Serving:	1
Calories:	250
Fat grams:	1.0
% of Fat:	3%

Carob Cake Frosting

    2¼ cups water
    2¼ cups maple syrup
    ½ teaspoon salt
    4½ tablespoons kuzu dissolved in 4½ tablespoons cold
        water (arrowroot can be substituted)
    4½ tablespoons vanilla
    ¾ teaspoon butterscotch or rum extract
    2¼ cups chopped toasted pecans (save 8–10 for
        decorating)
    2¼ cups medium flaked coconut (optional)

1. Heat water, syrup, and salt. Add dissolved kuzu and remaining ingredients to hot mixture and stir until thickened. Let cool before applying to cake.

2. Apply frosting between and on top of cooled cake layers.

3. Decorate with whole pecans.

Serving:	1
Calories:	330
Fat grams:	15.0
% of Fat:	41%

BASIC "CHEEZE" CAKE

(serves 8)

21   ounces silken "lite" tofu, extra firm
⅓   cup frozen unsweetened white grape juice
       concentrate
2   teaspoons vanilla
2   tablespoons arrowroot
       Pinch of salt
1   Graham Cracker Crust (See Index)
2   cups Fruit Topping (See Index)

1. Preheat oven to 350 degrees.

2. Combine all ingredients except crust in a food processor and blend for 2 minutes or until smooth.

3. Pour mixture into graham cracker crust and bake for 45 minutes or until a knife inserted into the center comes out clean.

4. Cool thoroughly before placing fruit topping over top of "cheeze" part of the cake.

5. Cover with plastic wrap, placing toothpicks to keep from messing up the top. Refrigerate for at least 2 hours.

Helpful Hint

If you make this "cheeze" cake the day before serving, its flavor will be more developed.

Serving:	1
Calories:	300
Fat grams:	4.0
% of Fat:	11%

GRAHAM CRACKER CRUST

(makes one 9" pie crust)

1¾ cups graham cracker crumbs
¼   cup Sucanat
⅓   cup WonderSlim or prune puree

1. Combine all ingredients in a food processor. *Do not over process.*

2. Press into a 9–inch lightly oiled pie pan.

Serving:	1
Calories:	135
Fat grams:	4.0
% of Fat:	25%

ITALIAN "CHEEZE" CAKE

(serves 8)

2¼ lbs. "lite" tofu, extra firm
1   lemon rind, grated
¾   cup honey
1½ teaspoons lemon juice
2½ teaspoons vanilla
     Dash of salt
2   slices dried pineapple, chopped
1   Graham Cracker Crust (See Index)

1. Preheat oven to 350 degrees.

2. Combine all ingredients except pineapple and crust in a food processor and beat for 2 minutes or until smooth.

3. Stir in pineapple.

4. Pour mixture into graham cracker crust and bake for 45 minutes or until a knife inserted into the center comes out clean.

Serving:	1
Calories:	280
Fat grams:	4.5
% of Fat:	14%

LEMON MOUSSE

(makes 1 quart; serves 8)

3   cups pineapple juice
½   cup orange juice concentrate
½   cup arrowroot
6   tablespoons honey, to taste
½   teaspoon salt
1   tablespoon lemon rind (yellow part only)
6   tablespoons lemon juice
     Orange peel strips, for garnish

1. Combine all ingredients in a blender. Whiz until smooth.

2. Pour into saucepan and cook until thick, stirring constantly for 5–7 minutes.

3. Place in glass stemmed glasses and set in refrigerator to sit overnight. Garnish with orange peel strips and/or mint leaves.

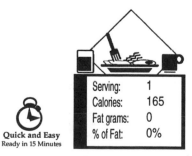

Quick and Easy
Ready in 15 Minutes

Serving:	1
Calories:	165
Fat grams:	0
% of Fat:	0%

SWEET POTATO ORANGE CUPS

(serves 6)

Serve as a dessert or snack.

Oranges (½ per serving)
Baked sweet potatoes (or yams)
Cinnamon
Nutmeg
Fresh mint leaves

1. Cut oranges in half (fancy if you wish); juice, and remove meat with spoon. Save the juice.
2. Bake yams until done and scoop out into bowl, then mix with cinnamon and nutmeg and add enough orange juice to make smooth. (Use hand or electric mixer, or a food processor.)
3. Spoon yam mixture into orange peels, using a fork to decorate.
4. Garnish with fresh mint leaf, and chill.

Helpful Hint

Measurements, of course, depend on the size and quantity of oranges and yams. For this purpose, 3 cups of cooked yams use ½ tablespoon cinnamon, ½ teaspoon nutmeg, and 2 tablespoons of orange juice.

Serving:	1
Calories:	135
Fat grams:	0
% of Fat:	2%

PEACH COBBLER

(serves 8)

Top with nondairy frozen dessert.

Crust

- 1 cup rolled oats
- 1 cup whole wheat flour
- ½ cup Grapenuts cereal
- 1 teaspoon cinnamon
- 1 cup unsweetened apple juice concentrate

Filling

- 6 cups fresh ripe peaches, sliced
- 1 teaspoon vanilla
- 1 teaspoon lemon rind, grated
- 3 tablespoons arrowroot
- ½ cup raisins (optional)
- 1 cup unsweetened apple juice concentrate

1. To make the topping, combine dry ingredients. Stir in apple juice concentrate until mixture holds together.

2. Mix all filling ingredients together in a bowl and toss lightly. Place in a glass baking dish.

3. Crumble topping evenly over peaches, making sure to cover the entire surface.

4. Cover and bake at 375 degrees for 30 minutes.

5. Uncover and bake for another 20 minutes, allowing top to get brown and crispy.

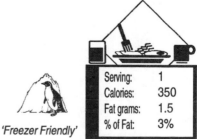

'Freezer Friendly'

Serving:	1
Calories:	350
Fat grams:	1.5
% of Fat:	3%

POACHED PEARS

(serves 6)

6   bosc or comice pears
3   cups black cherry juice
1   teaspoon vanilla (preferably bourbon)
3½" strips lemon peel (yellow part)
2   tablespoons arrowroot (optional)

1. Peel pears, cut in half and core.

2. Bring juice and lemon peel to a boil.

3. Add pears and cook gently until translucent around the edges. Add vanilla.

4. Dissolve 2 tablespoons arrowroot in ¼ cup cherry juice (or water) and add to juice to thicken (optional). Serve hot or cover and chill.

Quick and Easy
Ready in 15 Minutes

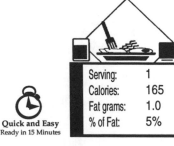

Serving:	1
Calories:	165
Fat grams:	1.0
% of Fat:	5%

RICH MOIST FRUITCAKE

(makes one loaf; serves 8)

1   cup carrots, grated
1   cup raisins
½   cup honey
¼   cup dates, chopped
1   teaspoon cinnamon
1   teaspoon allspice
½   teaspoon nutmeg
¼   teaspoon ground cloves
1¾ cups water
1½ cups whole wheat flour
1   teaspoon baking soda
½   cup bran
½   cup chopped walnuts (optional)

1. Cook carrots, raisins, dates, honey and spices in water for 10 minutes. Let cool.

2. Mix and sift together flour, baking soda and bran and then add walnuts, if used.

3. Add to carrot mixture and mix well.

4. Pour into a lightly oiled loaf pan, or 9 x 9 inch baking dish.

5. Bake at 325 degrees for 45 minutes.

Options

Substitute grated zucchini or apple for the carrots.

Substitute prunes or figs for the raisins,
or use all of the dates.

Serving:	1
Calories:	230
Fat grams:	1.0
% of Fat:	4%

SUMPTUOUS APPLE PIE

(serves 8)

Crust

    2   cups whole wheat pastry flour
    ¾   cup finely ground almonds
    1   cup apple juice, cold

1. Add flour and almonds to food processor and add apple juice slowly while processing into a ball (should be sticky).
2. Roll out half of dough for crust and place in lightly oiled pie pan. From remaining dough, make strips for top of the pie.

Filling

         Apricot preserves (optional)
    12   cups red delicious or granny smith apples, peeled, cored, and thinly sliced
    1   tablespoon lemon juice
    ½   teaspoon cinnamon
    ½   teaspoon nutmeg
    ½   cup apple juice
    ¼   cup Sucanat
    3   tablespoons arrowroot
         Raisins (optional)

1. Put apricot preserves in thin layer on bottom of uncooked pie crust.
2. Combine all other filling ingredients in a medium-sized saucepan and cover. Slowly, and on low heat, simmer about 10 minutes, stirring often. *Be careful not to burn.* Apples should be only slightly tender.
3. Place apples, raisins and sauce in pie shell with a large spoon. Criss-cross top with pastry strips.

Bake at 375 degrees, covered with foil, for one hour.

    4. Remove foil and brown the crust for 5 minutes at 400 degrees.

    5. Allow pie to cool for 10 minutes before cutting.

Helpful Hint

Brush top with orange juice before baking for glaze.

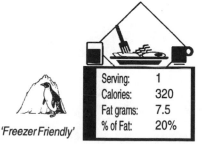

'Freezer Friendly'

Serving:	1
Calories:	320
Fat grams:	7.5
% of Fat:	20%

SWEET BISCUITS

(makes 12 biscuits)

Serve plain or with your favorite spread or fruit sauce.

2	cups whole wheat pastry flour
1	teaspoon (rounded) baking powder
½	teaspoon baking soda
1	teaspoon Sucanat
½	teaspoon salt
1	teaspoon cinnamon
1¼	cup soy milk (or rice milk)
1	teaspoon vanilla

1. Place dry ingredients in bowl.

2. Add milk and vanilla to center of ingredients. Carefully fold from center to the outside until all ingredients are combined. *Do not over stir!*

3. Drop by tablespoons onto nonstick, lightly oiled, cookie sheet.

4. Bake at 400 degrees for 10 minutes, until golden.

'Freezer Friendly'

Serving:	1
Calories:	80
Fat grams:	1.0
% of Fat:	11%

TOFU FROSTING

(serves 8)

Use on cakes or muffins.

8   ounces "lite" tofu (extra firm)
4   tablespoons rice syrup
1   teaspoon vanilla extract
½   teaspoon cardamom
Optional: orange or almond extract in place of vanilla
     and cardamom.

1. Blend all ingredients in a food processor or blender until smooth.

Serving:	1
Calories:	40
Fat grams:	0
% of Fat:	8%

Quick and Easy
Ready in 15 Minutes

YAM PIE

(serves 8)

Crust (makes 2 pie crusts)

2   cups whole wheat pastry flour
¾   cup finely ground almonds
¾   cup apple juice, cold

1. Add flour and almonds to food processor and add apple juice slowly while processing into a ball (should be sticky).
2. Roll out half for crust and place in lightly oiled pie pan. Wrap other half in plastic wrap and freeze.

Filling

3   large yams (approximately 4 cups)
¼   cup whole wheat pastry flour or spelt flour
¼   cup honey or brown rice syrup
1   tablespoon cinnamon
⅛   teaspoon ground cardamom
½   teaspoon allspice
¼   teaspoon salt

1. Preheat oven to 400 degrees. Wash and poke holes in yams. Bake until tender, approximately 1 hour, depending on size of yams. Let yams cool, then peel while still slightly warm.
2. Puree with all other ingredients in a food processor or blender.
3. Pour mixture into pie crust and bake uncovered for approximately 1 hour at 350 degrees.
4. Chill thoroughly before slicing.
5. Top with tofu or nut cream or serve plain. Garnish with orange peel strips. Wait until after the pie cools before garnishing.

Serving:	1
Calories:	255
Fat grams:	6.0
% of Fat:	20%

Helpful Hints

FOOD TIPS

One of the best ways to maintain a healthy diet is to have healthy food easily available. The following are helpful steps that I follow and recommend.

Apples:

To avoid discoloring, rub a little lemon juice on the exposed flesh or drop the apple slices in a bowl of water with lemon juice. If you don't have lemons, dunk the apple pieces in slightly salted water until you are ready to use them. If you like the taste, submerging them in pineapple juice will also work.

Beans:

The ideal way to prepare beans is to buy organic dry beans in bulk at your local natural food store. Sort them to remove any stones, and soak them overnight in three times their volume of water. Drain them in the morning and cover them again with three times their volume of fresh water. Cook them for the proper amount of time.

If time is a factor, you can purchase cooked canned beans at the supermarket. Make sure they are not packed in oil, and rinse them to remove any added salt.

One of the best ways to always have cooked beans on hand is to double or triple the amount needed in the recipe and freeze the leftover cooked beans. I always have plastic quart containers or quart size plastic bags filled with assorted kinds of cooked beans. A great time saver!

Eggplant:

If you want to prevent eggplant from tasting bitter, remove the skin. Slice the eggplant first, then cut the skin off with scissors. To prevent eggplant from discoloring, drop it into salted water until you are ready to cook it.

Flour, storing:

When storing flours unrefrigerated, place a handful of bay leaves in with the flour to keep bugs away. (I have no idea why it works, but it does.)

Fruit, ripening:

To help speed up the ripening of mangoes, store them in a paper bag in a dark, warm place. A ripe mango is bright yellow-orange. Nectarines and pears will also ripen in one or two days in a paper bag.

Garlic:

Purchase either one or three pound containers of peeled fresh garlic (membership clubs or some supermarkets). As soon as you get home, process all of the garlic in a food processor until finely minced. Place in small plastic containers, label, date, and freeze. One clove of garlic is equivalent to one teaspoon of minced garlic. When your freezer reserve gets down to one container, get another big jar. Be careful not to buy prepared garlic that is stored in oil.

Grapefruits & Oranges:

If you want the white part of the grapefruit or orange to come off easily, dunk the whole fruit into hot water for two minutes before peeling. The white will tear away with the peel. If you want, you can loosen the peel, then refrigerate.

Herbs & Spices:

It would be ideal if we could use only fresh herbs all the time, but of course this is not reality. So, here is the formula to convert fresh herbs to dried, or the reverse.

When a recipe calls for fresh herbs and you want to use dried, cut the amount in half because dried herbs are concentrated. The same is true in reverse – when substituting fresh for dried, double the amount.

When using dried herbs, use a mortar and pestle or a Japanese suribachi to bring out the flavors. If you don't have one, at least put the dried herbs between your hands and do what I call "Robert's rub."

Loaves & Burgers:

The trick to making loaves and burgers hold together is in the moisture of the mix. It should be sticky, but not too wet or dry. It is helpful to know that you are in charge of the moisture and can adjust it either way. If the mixture feels too wet, you can absorb the excess moisture by adding some bread crumbs or oats. If it is too dry, just add more tamari or any other liquid the recipe suggests.

Onions:

To avoid crying when peeling onions, place them in the freezer for ten minutes before chopping. Do not remove the core end of the onion so the juices will be reduced and so will the tears. Some prefer to peel onions under water.

Oranges & Lemons, zest:

To zest an orange or lemon, use the fine shredding disk on a food processor. Place the orange or lemon into the large feed tube. Lock the sleeve of the pusher in place over the fruit. Unlock the pusher and hold it up, preventing it from touching the fruit. Allow the orange or lemon to "dance" in the feed tube while the machine is running. This action produces a fine zest which will fall into the work bowl.

Pasta:

What an exciting adventure awaits you the first time you wander away from the supermarket semolina and into the pasta section of a good natural food store! Face it, white spaghetti, like the white flour it's made from, has very little taste, which is why it seems to require rich, fatty sauces to have any appeal. But here you'll find pastas made not only from whole wheat flour, but with buckwheat, spinach, carrots, varied grains and their sprouts, and even some exotic (and possibly unknown to you) ingredients such as amaranth flour. And, as long as you *read the labels* carefully, they'll all provide you with the same health benefits – low fat, low sodium, high fiber – while offering a variety of tastes, textures and appearances to make your cooking anything but dull, not only gastronomically but visually as well.

If you're shopping for pasta in a regular supermarket, read the label and look for pasta made without eggs, and preferably with whole wheat, corn or spinach.

Potatoes:

Always have cooked baked potatoes on hand. Scrub and wash the potatoes, then prick each one with a fork. For 15–20 potatoes, bake at 450° until soft, about 60 minutes depending upon the size of the potatoes. Let cool. Place all the potatoes in an *open* gallon-size plastic bag and store them in the refrigerator.

To reheat a potato as a meal or snack, place it in a toaster oven (to get crispy) or heat it up in the microwave for one minute. Generally, I either slice them open and put salsa or Spike on top, or leave them whole for munching in the car when I'm in a hurry. When the bag gets down to a couple of potatoes, repeat the process. This way, you will always have a tasty, healthy snack available.

Rice:

I use an electric nonstick rice cooker and cook a full load every time (it makes 4 quarts) because rice freezes well. Make a large pot of long or short grain brown rice, dump it into a large bowl, toss and let cool. Take quart size plastic bags and fill them with the cooked rice. Stack them flat so they will take up less room in the freezer. Always keep one or two bags in the refrigerator for immediate use. When you run low on the rice in the refrigerator, take more out of the freezer and let it defrost in the refrigerator.

When you steam vegetables, just put some cooked rice on top of them. The rice will regain moisture while it heats. You can also place some chili, marinara, stew, etc., on top of the cold rice and zap for 2–3 minutes in the microwave for a quick, healthy meal.

Salads & Vegetables:

Admit it... when you get home after work or a full day of activities, it is a real chore to start making a salad from scratch. The trouble with not having salad available is that it is easier to skip it when you are tired or in a hurry. Here's what I recommend:

After you get home from the market, put your fresh produce away in the refrigerator and immediately wash the romaine lettuce (romaine has the most nutrients, iceberg has none), spin dry, cut into bite size pieces, and place in a large bowl. Next, wash, dry and slice up celery stalks, and add them to the bowl of lettuce. Take a red cabbage, chop to your preference in size (I like thicker slices, you may like thin) and add to the bowl. Toss all the ingredients and place into a gallon size plastic storage bag. Close it tightly and put in the refrigerator.

The next day when you get home, instead of fussing, just grab a couple of handfuls of salad, place in a salad bowl with some sliced tomatoes, sprouts, red pepper or other favorite vegetable. Add some oil-free salad dressing and *oo la la!*

The same principal applies to vegetables. Take cauliflower or broccoli, trim and place in plastic bags. When you get home, all you have to do is get the steamer boiling, rinse the vegetables, and place in a steamer basket with some cooked rice.

For healthy snacks, always keep peeled carrots and celery sticks in a bowl of water in the refrigerator. Grab a handful and put them in a small plastic bag to keep in the car for munchies.

Salt:

The ideal salt to use is sea salt or kosher salt. These salts do not contain the additives that make it free-flowing, or added iodine. Therefore they do not have that "metallic" taste that often accompanies regular supermarket salt.

Smelly Foods:

If the house starts smelling as you cook certain vegetables like broccoli or brussels sprouts, put a piece of red pepper into the pot. If you do not have red pepper, use a piece of bread, preferably rye, which works especially well with cabbage and cauliflower. Turnips will smell a lot less if you add one teaspoon of sugar to the cooking water.

Spices, hot:

For spices like cayenne or crushed red pepper, or hot sauces like tabasco, remember Robert's motto: "You can always add, but you cannot take away!"

Vegetarian "Chicken" & "Beef" Broth Powders:

Many recipes call for vegetarian "chicken" and "beef" broth powder. These powders are available at most natural food stores and, although they contain a trace of safflower oil, are wonderful ingredients to have available in your kitchen. They usually contain hydrolyzed soy protein, sea salt, herbs, nutritional yeast, parsley, spices, and vegetables. They taste like chicken and/or beef; however, they contain no meat. We have a recipe for Chicken-Style Seasoning that also tastes like chicken flavor, but contains no oil. These are real flavor enhancers, so make sure your kitchen is well supplied.

Whole Wheat Pastry Flour:

Whole wheat pastry flour works best in muffin, quick bread, cake and cookie recipes calling for whole wheat flour. Regular whole wheat flour may be used with good results, but whole wheat pastry flour produces lighter, softer textured baked goods.

COOKING TIPS

Baking (instead of stove top cooking):

Many times when a recipe calls for cooking a large quantity of tomato sauce, stew, or a bean and vegetable dish, the best way to cook it is to bake it. Baking in the oven generates "radiated" heat rather than direct heat to the bottom of the pot. This way it won't burn or scorch the food on the bottom of a large pot and undercook the food on top.

Boiling:

To avoid running out of water when steaming vegetables, put a handful of marbles in the water. If the water level gets too low, the marbles will start rattling, telling you to add more.

Converting Recipes:

Ok, you have a favorite recipe that you know is not healthy, but you love the taste and it has become a "comfort" food. So how can we convert it so you don't feel deprived while you are making the transition to a healthier lifestyle?

There is good news and bad news. First, the bad. You probably can't duplicate recipes that contain high-fat and -cholesterol ingredients such as meats, dairy products or egg yolks to your satisfaction.

The good news is that many foods have flavors, textures and tastes close enough to the old high-fat foods to satisfy you. You will also discover many new foods that you never tasted before, which will expand your taste horizons.

Keep in mind that most people have maybe ten favorite dishes that they eat, over and over, all year. The trick now is to find the ten new dishes that most closely satisfy your new way of eating and support your choice to feel and look healthy all the time.

Cheese is one of those foods that many people have difficulty accepting alternatives. After a time, however, you will not miss the original because your taste buds will be satisfied by the new healthier substitutes, such as Vegetable Lasagna (made with tofu ricotta "cheeze") and Italian "Cheeze" Cake. After eating pizza just a couple of times without cheese and sprinkled with nutritional yeast, you will notice that it tastes very satisfying.

Recently, I saw a recipe on television that sounded really interesting because it used mung beans, which I had never used before. The recipe called for sautéing (in olive oil, of course) onions, garlic, etc., and after the beans were cooked, adding about two pounds of pork cubes. "Delicious!" said the show host. I scribbled down all the ingredients, took them into the office, and on the computer imagined myself in the kitchen cooking the recipe with my revisions.

Naturally, I used vegetarian chicken-style broth powder stock instead of chicken stock to sauté the onions and garlic. I cooked the mung beans after they soaked overnight and added them to the sautéed veggies. Then I peeled, cubed and steamed 2¼ pounds of potatoes (instead of the pork cubes) and added them to the cooked bean mixture. The dish was delicious, but needed some color. So the next time I made it I added one cup of diced carrots and some celery. When it was tested by others, it proved to be an unusual and hearty casserole that I welcomed to my repertoire.

The primary thing to change in recipes you want to convert is to eliminate sautéing in oil. Next, think of ways to substitute beans, grains, potatoes or vegetables for meat. When sauces or gravies are given body with oil, remember we have ways of thickening and adding "mouth feel" without all that fat.

You will find after a few months that you will be discovering recipes in magazines that are "convertible" and surprising friends and family alike. Remember, don't tell them it's healthy – just serve up your new recipe!

Freezer Friendly:

One of the most important ways to stay with a program of healthy eating is to always have delicious, healthy food available. The best way to do this is to create your own "T.V. dinners" and to always have enough food in the freezer to accommodate unexpected guests.

So every time you set out to do some cooking, remember to cook enough for at least two meals, not one. I would never think of cooking one loaf; I always make at least two loaves, plus another to make into burgers. Eat one for dinner and freeze one loaf and the burgers for future meals.

The same is true for sauces like marinara, bolognese, and enchilada. Make the maximum quantity of sauce, use what you need, and freeze the rest in plastic containers labeled with the contents and date.

Many of the dips, sauces, soups, gravies and other dishes can be frozen for future meals. Gravies to be thickened with arrowroot or cornstarch should be frozen before the thickening, as they have a tendency to need rethickening when they are reheated.

Always use the FIFO method (first in, first out). That way you will always have fresh frozen foods available.

Basic Knife Skills:

Your knives are an extension of your hands, so you must treat them with respect and care. A dull knife is dangerous because it makes you work harder and use too much pressure. A sharp knife is safe and can last for many years.

Never put your knives in a dishwasher! Keep them separate from each other or any other utensils. Use a knife storage block. If they are stored with other tools, the blades will get nicked.

Use a sharpening steel often. It quickly realigns and hones the edge. Then you will not have to sharpen the blade too often. The sharpening steel is magnetic and will attract metal particles which are worn off the blade during the sharpening. For this reason, you should always wipe the blade after using the steel.

If your knives are in poor condition, bring them to a professional knife sharpener.

Measurements:
- 1 medium onion = 1 ½ cups
- 1 clove garlic = 1 teaspoon minced garlic
- Generally, one pound of a chopped vegetable (e.g., onion, carrot, zucchini) = 1 quart

Liquid Measures	Dry Measures

Liquid Measures
- 1 Tablespoon = 3 Teaspoons
- 2 Tablespoons = 1 Oz.
- 1 Cup = 8 Oz. or ½ Pint
- 2 Cups = 16 Oz. or 1 Pint
- 4 Cups = 32 Oz. or 1 Quart
- 16 Cups = 4 Quarts or 1 Gallon

Dry Measures
- A Pinch or Dash = ⅛ tsp.
- 3 Teaspoons = 1 Tablespoon
- 4 Tablespoons = ¼ Cup
- 5⅓ Tablespoons = ⅓ Cup
- 16 Oz. = 1 Lb.

Sautéing:

One of the prime ways to decrease fat in preparing food is to eliminate the use of all oils. I know, this sounds radical! That was exactly my reaction the first time I saw that suggestion. As I read all of the information and studies about how harmful oil – even vegetable oil – is in comparison to the claimed benefits, I realized I needed to avoid it.

Now the question was, what effect would it have on cooking delicious food? The answer is that many dishes are quite delicious when substituting vegetable stock, tamari, apple juice or just plain water for oil. In fact, when making any tomato-based sauce, sautéing in apple juice eliminates the acidic taste of tomatoes. My Italian neighbor used to add sugar to tomato sauce to help dissipate the acid. By sautéing in natural apple juice, we take care of both the acid and oil problems.

Soup Too Salty:

If your soup is too salty, put in a couple of thin slices of raw potato. When they become translucent, remove them. They should absorb the salt. If appropriate, add a can of tomatoes. They are sufficiently bland to use up the excess salt. Adding a couple of pinches of brown sugar also tends to mask the saltiness.

Stews & Sauces, burned:

Without scraping any of the stuck part, use a wooden spoon to transfer the unburned stew or sauce to another pot immediately. Add more onion, which tends to overcome any remaining burned flavor. If it still has a burned taste, cover the pot with a damp cloth and let stand for half an hour. If it is still unpleasant, salvage the dish by adding Liquid Smoke or barbecue sauce and rename the dish "country style."

WEIGHT LOSS TIPS

➪ If you're trying to lose weight, it's essential to eliminate high-fat plant foods, such as avocado, coconut, olives and all vegetable oils. After all, oil is liquid fat. You also want to eliminate nuts, nut butters (such as almond and peanut butter), seeds, seed butters (such as tahini), and soybean products, such as tofu. Yes, tofu *is* health food – but it's higher fat health food than you may need. Regular tofu is 54% fat; "lite" tofu is still 30% fat. Use it sparingly (who eats a slab of tofu, anyway?) or save it for special occasions.

➪ For most rapid weight loss, do not include the optional higher-fat ingredients in some of the recipes, such as nuts (or nut butter or nut milk), seeds, or tahini.

➪ If you want the flavor of nut or seed butter, here's a trick for reducing the fat. When you purchase a jar of almond butter, peanut butter or tahini, you'll notice an inch or so of oil sitting on top of the butter. Instead of mixing it in, pour the oil off. That will make it harder to spread, but lighter in fat. If you are using a recipe that calls for tahini, you can eliminate the seed butter. The dip won't be as rich, but you will be surprised how tasty it will be.

MENU PLANNING TIPS

↝ Use foods as close to their natural whole state as possible.

↝ Try to serve foods grown without chemical fertilizers or pesticides whenever possible.

↝ Choose locally grown produce, or at least grown in a similar climate zone, and use what is freshest and in season.

↝ Use starches such as grains, corn, potatoes, sweet potatoes, and beans as your main staple, with the addition of fresh fruits and vegetables.

↝ Serve a variety of foods in each meal.

↝ Use the new USDA Food Guide Pyramid to arrive at the proper balance of the basic food groups.

↝ First choose the main focus of a meal, generally some form of starch. Next, choose the complementary foods from among the fresh vegetables that are in season, keeping in mind color combinations and contrasts in texture and shape.

↝ Remember to think in terms of volume when preparing all labor intensive dishes. Large quantities allow for the creative use of leftovers and for freezing for future use.

MENU PLANNING TIPS

USDA Food Guide Pyramid (1992)

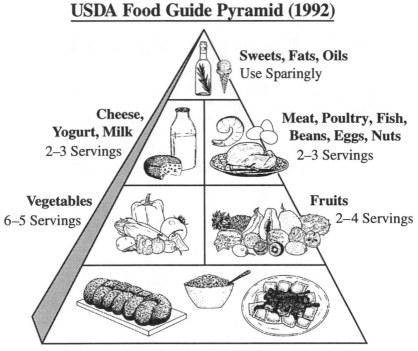

Sweets, Fats, Oils
Use Sparingly

Cheese, Yogurt, Milk
2–3 Servings

Meat, Poultry, Fish, Beans, Eggs, Nuts
2–3 Servings

Vegetables
6–5 Servings

Fruits
2–4 Servings

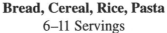

Bread, Cereal, Rice, Pasta
6–11 Servings

FOOD LABELING

If food labels seem so confusing that you don't even bother reading them, you're not alone. We asked fitness expert, author and lecturer Joan Price for help. Here's her explanation from her new book, *Joan Price Says, Yes, You CAN Get In Shape!*

Confused by trying to decode food labels? They do provide essential information for making wise choices. But you have to be careful and learn how to read them, or you'll be misled into thinking a food item is healthier than it is!

Here's the important information you need to know: **What percent of the calories are from fat?** In other words, the item is what percent fat? Some food items make this easy – usually foods with nothing to hide! They list "calories from fat" and some number that you hope is 20% or less.

Most food items, however, do not tell you this, although you can figure it out. They give you the information they're required by law to disclose, and no more.

Be wary: you'll see a "%" number, and it will be very low. Don't be fooled into thinking that's the percent of calories from fat – read the fine print! Grab a food label now and follow along with me. See the heading "%DV*"? Now read the teensy print at the bottom: "Percent Daily Values (DV) are based on a 2,000 calorie diet."

What does *that* mean, you ask. Here's the tricky part. They are telling you the percentage of a *full day's fat intake* that you'll get from this one serving of this food item *if* you are eating 2,000 calories a day, and *if* you want to keep your fat intake to 30% of your calories! In other words, on a 2,000 calorie diet at 30% fat, this serving will give you __% of your *daily* fat.

This is better than no information, I suppose, but not by much. First of all, you probably aren't aiming for a 2,000 calorie diet, and even if you are, 30% fat is too high for optimum health and weight management. Besides, how many of us choose individual food items based on the whole day's allotment of fat, or understand how to compare foods on that basis?

My recommendation: ignore that "%DV" number completely, and use this formula instead. **Take the number of grams of fat ("total fat") in whatever serving size they give, multiply by nine (because there are nine calories in a gram of fat), then divide by the total calories in that serving size.** The result will be the percent of calories from fat, exactly the figure you want to know. It doesn't matter what serving size is given; the percentage from fat is the same.

For optimum health, weight control and energy, try to choose items that are 20% or below, or ideally, 10%. If you buy a higher fat item, try to use it sparingly – a light sprinkling rather than a chunk or a slab. Yes, some respected health organizations do recommend a 30% fat diet (which means 30% of your calories come from fat). But if you pin them down off the record, many times they'll admit that 20% is better, but they don't think the American public would accept a lower figure! Nonsense! If you know you'll be healthier, slimmer and more energetic if you reduce your calories from fat to 20% or under, wouldn't you give it a try?

(From *Joan Price Says, Yes, You CAN Get In Shape!* (Pacifica Press, 1996, order from Unconventional Moves, 1-888-BFITTER(234-8837), reprinted by permission.)

Let's use Joan's formula and look at olives: 25 calories, 2.5 g total fat, %DV = 4%. Now let's do the calculation. Olives have 2.5 g total fat; and 25 total calories. 2.5 x 9 = 22.5, divided by 25 = .9 = 90%. Olives derive 90% of their calories from fat. Is this a healthy food? Not in my book!

Glossary of Natural Foods
& Unusual Ingredients

A GLOSSARY OF
NATURAL FOODS &
UNUSUAL INGREDIENTS

Agar-Agar:

A vegetarian gelatin substitute derived from various species of red algae. It is sold in sticks or flakes and used like ordinary gelatin. The flake form yields the most consistent results; the powder undergoes more processing. One tablespoon of flakes will jell one cup of liquid. To use, let the agar-agar soften in cold liquid and then slowly simmer. *Don't boil.* Stir the mixture occasionally until the agar dissolves. It will set at room temperature. Agar-agar has almost no taste and, because it mostly consists of indigestible fiber, virtually no calories. Available in natural food stores and Asian markets.

Amazake:

A sweet, fermented brown rice nectar, amazake is used as a sweetener or sweet beverage. It is not a refined sweetener, but is concentrated and naturally sweet, and is milder than honey or maple. Originally from Japan, it is now made in this country and is available in natural food stores.

Arrowroot:

A starchy flour made from the root of the West Indian plant of the same name and used as a thickening agent. It is usually less processed than cornstarch, for which it can be substituted. Arrowroot will keep indefinitely if stored in an airtight container in a cool, dry place. Sold in supermarkets in the spice section (not the baking supply aisle), natural food stores, and Asian and Caribbean markets.

Balsamic Vinegar:

The Italians developed this now *haute* dark-brown vinegar. It's made from grapes with a high sugar content. The mellow sweet-sour flavor makes it good in vinaigrette salad dressings or splashed on freshly steamed vegetables. Balsamic vinegar is rather expensive, but a little goes a long way. Like all vinegars, it will keep indefinitely if stored in an airtight container; it need not be refrigerated. Available in natural food stores and gourmet groceries.

Basmati Rice:

A special variety of long grain rice with a fluffy texture, nutty taste and an aroma of buttered peanuts. Basmati originated in the foothills of the Himalayas. It is usually imported from India or Pakistan, where it is milled into white rice. Basmati is now grown in the United States, often organically. It can be used like ordinary long or medium grain rice, but it is especially good in Indian recipes with aromatic spices. Whole brown, as opposed to polished, basmati is available in natural food stores.

Bragg Liquid Aminos:

An all purpose seasoning, developed by Paul C. Bragg as an alternative to tamari or soy sauce. It is made from soybeans and water and contains no preservatives, coloring agents, additives, alcohol, chemicals, MSG, or added salt. Available in natural food stores and some supermarkets.

Brown Rice Syrup:

This natural sweetener is prepared by adding dried sprouted barley or barley enzymes to cooked rice and fermenting the mixture until the rice starch breaks down to complex sugars. Like barley malt syrup, rice syrup is only moderately sweet, and its sugars are gradually absorbed by the body rather than producing a sudden sugar high. Available in natural food stores.

Brown Rice Vinegar:

A mildly sweet vinegar made from fermented brown rice. Used extensively in Japanese or Chinese cuisine, rice vinegar enhances the flavor of plain rice. It is good in salad dressings and soy-based dips and sauces. It's also an excellent pickling agent. Brown rice vinegar is available in natural food stores; the rice vinegar sold in Asian markets is usually white.

Traditionally brewed, unfiltered rice vinegars often contain rice sediment that can make the liquid look cloudy. This cloudiness is no cause for concern; in fact it is a sign of high quality.

Capers:

Flower buds of a Mediterranean shrub, pickled and used as a condiment. Jarred capers are usually packed in salt water or vinegar. Their flavor is hard to describe, but capers add a delicate piquancy to dishes. Available in gourmet food stores and in many grocery stores, next to the more humble pickle.

Cardamom:

In the Orient these exceedingly aromatic seeds are called "Seeds of Paradise" and were carried to Europe from Asia over the old overland spice routes. In ancient Greek and Roman days, it was used mainly as a perfume. It is a member of the ginger family and grows prolifically on the Malabar coast of India, in Ceylon and, to a certain extent, in Mexico and Central America. We use the dried pods in our kitchens. The pods vary greatly in length and color, from almost white to a dark reddish-brown. Cardamom seeds are used in many Eastern dishes, particularly in Indian curries. Kashmiris use it to flavor tea, and the Arabs their coffee. They flavor liqueurs, cakes and pastries in Scandinavia, Germany and Russia. Available in the spice section of natural food stores and supermarkets.

Carob Powder:

A sweet powder made from the seed pods of a Mediterranean tree. It has a flavor similar to chocolate, but it contains less fat and no caffeine. Choose between the milder unroasted or the more intense, roasted varieties. Carob powder is less soluble than cocoa, and undissolved particles may remain in beverages or other foods. The powder will last for at least a year if stored in a closed container in a dry place; excess moisture will cause it to lump. Because carob is 46% natural sugars, recipes made with it require little additional sweetening. Available canned and in bulk in natural food stores and some supermarkets.

Chilies:

The immature pods of various peppers (including Anaheim, ancho, cayenne, jalapeno, poblano and serrano), used to add heat and color to dishes and to make sauces such as mole. A few chilies are relatively mild, but most are quite hot. Generally the smaller the chili, the hotter it is. Besides tasting hot, fresh chilies can burn your hands. Wear thin gloves while handling them and keep fingers away from your eyes until you have thoroughly washed your hands. Prepare fresh chilies for use by broiling them until blistered and then allowing them to steam for 15 minutes in a closed paper bag. Under cold running water, slip off the skin and remove the seeds and veins. Fresh green chilies are used in curries, chutney, pickles and salads. They will keep about a week in the refrigerator, or can be frozen or dried. Dried red chilies (ripe chilies that have been dried in the sun) are used in curries and soups. Both varieties are widely available at supermarkets, produce markets and Hispanic groceries.

Chipotle Chili:

Chipotles are jalapeno peppers slow dried over a wood fire. Their seductive smoky aroma is usually featured in sauces, but there are easier, faster ways to use them, too. Try this – if you're cooking rice, add a chipotle to the water and it will taste like you grilled your rice. Do the same with pasta, flavor the water, then discard. You can also do this when steaming hard vegetables. Chipotle chilies will be available in Hispanic groceries, some natural food stores or markets that cater to Hispanic customers.

Cilantro:

The parsley-like leaves of fresh coriander, also called Mexican, Spanish, or Chinese parsley. Cilantro lends a unique, zesty flavor that some love and others abhor. (One author wrote that it tastes like soap.) Buy it fresh because the flavor dissipates when the herb is dried. The dried cilantro on the spice shelf won't add much taste to your cooking. Cilantro is widely used in Mexican and Indian cuisine, and to a lesser extent in Asian and Hispanic. Available at most produce stands and markets.

Dijon Mustard:

(Say *dee-ZHOHN.*) Hailing originally from Dijon, France, this grayish-yellow mustard is known for its clean, sharp flavor, which can range from mild to hot. Dijon is made from brown and black mustard seeds, white wine, unfermented grape juice and various seasonings.

Egg Replacer:

A combination of starches and leavening agents used to replace the leavening and/or binding qualities of eggs in baking. Egg replacer is a dry product and cannot be used to make scrambled eggs or omelets. Most commercially available replacers contain egg whites, along with nonfat dry milk powder, corn oil, lecithin, artificial flavorings, preservatives and/or colorings. Vegan egg replacers are made from tapioca, potato starch, vegetable lecithin, calcium carbonate and cellulose-based filler. Thanks to the cholesterol controversy, egg replacers are available everywhere.

Emes Kosher-Gel:

A plain parave gelatin powder, unflavored and unsweetened. It contains no meat or dairy. It does contain carrageenan, locust bean gum and malto-dextrin. Use one tablespoon per each pint of liquid. It is available in natural food stores and kosher markets.

Fagioli:

(Say *fa-ZHOH-lee.*) The Italian word for "beans," usually white kidney beans. String beans are called fagiolini.

FruitSource:

An all-purpose sweetener made of grape juice concentrate and whole rice syrup. It comes in liquid and granular form and can be used cup for cup where honey or sugar is required. Available in natural food stores.

Garam Masala:

It literally means "hot mixture" and is the principal spice blend of north Indian cookery. There are as many versions as there are cooks. Garam masala is always used sparingly. The spices are usually dry roasted and are a blend of cinnamon sticks, bay leaves, cumin seeds, coriander seeds, cardamom, peppercorns, cloves and mace. The proportions change to suit your taste and the dish. Available in natural food stores and Indian markets.

Ginger Root:

The fresh, knobby rootstock of the ginger plant, which is grated or sliced and used for seasoning. One tablespoon of freshly grated ginger (peeling is optional) equals 1/8 teaspoon of the dried, ground spice. Once found only in Asian groceries, ginger root is now in supermarkets and produce stands.

Gluten:

The principal protein in wheat, gluten becomes stretchy and elastic when wheat flour dough is kneaded. Spelt, barley, oats, rye and triticale also contain some gluten. Highly refined ground gluten, often called gluten flour, is sometimes added to low gluten dough for added rising power. Available in natural food stores.

Gomasio:

Prepare sesame gomasio by heating sesame seeds in a stainless or nonstick skillet. Shake pan, keeping the seeds moving and popping to avoid burning. Seeds will turn golden brown in color and give off a wonderful aroma. Remove seeds and crush them with a mortar and pestle or in a Japanese suribachi. Prepared gomasio is available in natural food stores.

Guar Gum:

Guar gum is a vegetable gum made from the guar plant. It is a thickener and stabilizer used in soft drinks, nondairy frozen desserts, salad dressings, sauces, frozen fruit, puddings, fruit drinks and many other foods. Guar gum is cold water soluble. It has a tendency to form clumps unless properly dispersed. It is used in a wide range of food items because of its water-binding capacity. As a soluble fiber, guar gum is useful in reducing serum cholesterol. It is still hard to find, but is becoming more available in natural food stores.

Herbamare:

An herbed seasoning salt made according to the original formula created by the Swiss naturopath, Dr. A. Vogel. It is prepared with fresh organic grown herbs and salt from which the moisture has been removed by a vacuum process, slowly and at a low temperature. Available in natural food stores.

Kombu:

(Say *KOM-bu*.) Wide, thick and dark green seaweed, sometimes called sea cabbage. Besides its use in making dashi, kombu strips can be added to fried rice or vegetables, sliced into soups and stews, shredded and used as seasoning, used to wrap foods, and added to legumes to soften and help cook faster. Available in natural food stores.

Kosher Salt:

An additive-free course-grained salt. It is ritually used by the Jewish in food preparation, as well as gourmet cooks who prefer its texture and flavor. Available in markets in the kosher section.

Kuzu:

Kuzu is the powdered root of the kuzu plant. It is used for both its thickening and medicinal properties. Like arrowroot, kuzu must be dissolved in cold water before adding to hot liquids. Use one–half the amount required for arrowroot. Because kuzu is so expensive, arrowroot is often substituted, however the superior jelling, translucence, and sparkle are unique to kuzu. Available in natural food stores.

Liquid Smoke:

A seasoning made from natural hickory smoke, vinegar, brown sugar, and other flavorings. Available in natural food stores and supermarkets.

Mirin:

A sweet Japanese cooking wine, the best mirin is naturally brewed from sweet brown rice, rice "koji" (a natural starter), and water. Use it in dressings, marinades, sauces, glazes, and vegetable and noodle dishes. Available in natural food stores and Asian markets.

Miso:

(Say *ME-so.*) Miso is to vegetarian cooking what beef bouillon or gravy is to a meat-centered diet. This salty, fermented paste is made from cooked, aged soybeans and usually grains. Thick and spreadable, it's used for flavoring a wide variety of dishes and for making soup bases. It can also replace salt in many recipes. Miso is available in natural food stores in several varieties. Dark miso tends to be saltier and have a stronger flavor than lighter varieties. Shiro, or white miso, has a pale yellow color and a mild, almost sweet taste. Miso will keep for several months when refrigerated in an air tight container. Available in natural food stores and Asian markets.

Nori:

(Say *NOR-ee.*) Black, brown or deep purple seaweed, sold in thin, crispy sheets. Nori (or as the Irish call it, "laver") is commonly rolled around rice balls and other foods, or crumbled as a garnish. Lightly toast nori for a few minutes before using; it will turn a bright olive green. Available in natural food stores and Asian markets.

Nutritional Yeast:

A dietary supplement and seasoning with a nutty, cheesy taste. It comes in flakes or powder. Do not confuse with brewers yeast. Available in natural food stores.

Pine Nuts:

Seeds from the pine cones of certain evergreens. Also called "pignolias" or "pinons." Their mild flavor, a combination of almond and pine, is enhanced by toasting. They are eaten as a snack (either raw, or roasted and salted), used to make pesto, or added to soups, cakes, casseroles and curries. Pine nuts will keep for about a year if the shells are not broken and the nuts are stored in a cool, dry place. Shelled nuts will keep for several months if refrigerated, although they may become a bit moist. They are rather expensive but can be used sparingly. Available in natural and gourmet food stores.

Ponzu:

Sweet and pungent condiment made from soy sauce, citrus juices and mirin. Great over grains and vegetables or for marinating tofu. Available in Asian markets and natural food stores.

Rice Noodles:

Long, thin, white Chinese noodles generally sold in cellophane bags. Available in Asian markets and natural food stores.

Rice Vinegar:

A mild vinegar made from rice. Excellent for salads and sauces.

Saffron:

The most expensive spice in the world, saffron costs ten times as much as vanilla and 50 times as much as cardamom. The dried, thread-like stigmas of the saffron crocus are so light, over 20,000 produce only 4 ounces and have to be handpicked. Saffron has a distinctive, tenacious aroma and a penetrating, bitter, but highly aromatic taste. A small amount will flavor a large dish and color it a brilliant gold. Available in natural food and gourmet stores.

Sake:

A Japanese rice wine, usually served warm. Also used as a flavoring ingredient.

Sea Salt:

The type used through the ages. Sea salt is the result of the evaporation of sea water, the more costly of the salt-making processes. It comes in fine-grained or larger crystals. Available in natural food stores and some markets.

Seitan:

(Say *say-tan*.) A food made from boiled or baked wheat gluten. It can be purchased as a mix, ready-made in jars or packages, or frozen. Available in natural food stores and Asian markets.

Soba Noodles:

Long, narrow Japanese noodles made from either 100 percent buckwheat flour, or a combination of buckwheat and unbleached or whole wheat flours. Soba comes in several varieties with varying percentages of buckwheat. Mugwort, green tea powder, or other ingredients are sometimes added for extra flavor. Some varieties are best in soups and sauces, while others are excellent sauteed in apple juice or served like spaghetti. Like other Japanese pastas, these noodles are eggless as well as lighter and less sticky than Italian pastas. Available in natural food stores and Asian markets.

Soy Milk:

A milky beverage made primarily from soybeans and water. Most soy milk is aseptically packaged to last almost indefinitely before opening. Once opened, it keeps for several weeks if refrigerated. Fresh soy milk, which can be made at home from whole soybeans, is much more perishable and should be refrigerated in a glass container. Even then, it lasts only about four days. A few powdered soy milks are available. Just mix with water for a beverage or use like powdered milk in cooking. Sold in natural food stores and supermarkets.

Also try the flavored malted soy milks. For a treat that rivals a thick milk shake, place in the freezer until not quite frozen. Available in natural food stores.

Here's how 8 ounces of soy milk stacks up nutritionally against cow's milk: similar protein – 3.4 grams per 100 grams – and no cholesterol. Soy milk contains somewhat more iron, niacin and thiamin than cow's milk, but less calcium, vitamin A and riboflavin.

Spike:

A brand of all-purpose natural seasoning created by gourmet nutritionist, Gaylord Hauser. A blend of 39 herbs, vegetables, spices and salt. Available in original and salt-free blends at natural food stores and most supermarkets.

Sucanat:

100% organic granulated cane juice from which the water has been evaporated. It is certified by independent testing to be free of pesticides, chemicals, preservatives, artificial ingredients or flow agents. Because nothing is added and only water is removed, Sucanat retains the vitamins, minerals and trace elements found naturally in the sugar cane plant. It can be used cup for cup wherever sugar is required. Available in natural food stores.

Suribachi:

The ceramic mortar from Japan with a serrated surface for grinding seeds, herbs or mixing sauces. The suribachi comes with a wooden pestle called a suricogi.

Spelt:

Among the first natural grains known to man, spelt is not wheat. It was grown in Europe more than 9,000 years ago and is ecologically the ideal grain. It is not a hybrid like wheat and can be grown without fertilizers, pesticides and insecticides. The spelt kernel is tightly surrounded by a very strong hull, which protects the grain against all types of pollutants in the air, even radioactive fallout. It also protects the grain during storage, assuring you of the freshest possible product after dehulling and milling. Spelt flour can be substituted in any recipe for wheat flour. It can be used for baking, cooking, pasta, pancake mixes or any other application of your choice. Available in natural food stores and some supermarkets.

Sweet Brown Rice:

A waxy short grain rice that is slightly sweeter than regular rice. It cooks into a very sticky mass and is used in sushi, rice balls, baby food cereal, traditional Oriental pastries, puddings, and other desserts. It is also used to make amazake, mirin and mochi. Sweet brown rice is available in natural food stores. The variety found in Oriental groceries is more likely to be refined.

Tahini:

(Say *tah-HEE-nee*.) A thick, smooth paste made of raw, hulled and ground sesame seeds. A Middle Eastern food, tahini is used as a spread and as an ingredient in dressings, sauces and desserts. It can also be used as an oil, egg or milk replacement in many recipes. An unopened jar of tahini holds for six or seven months. After opening, it will last four to five months when refrigerated. A close relative of tahini is sesame butter, made from toasted, rather than raw, sesame seeds. It is thicker and has a nuttier flavor than tahini. Available in natural food stores and supermarkets, in the kosher section.

Tamarind:

(Say *TAM-uh-rihnd*.) Also known as "Indian date," the tamarind is the fruit of a tall shade tree native to Asia and northern Africa and widely grown in India. Tamarind pulp concentrate is popular as a flavoring in East Indian and Middle Eastern cuisines much like lemon juice is in Western culture. It is used to season full-flavored foods such as chutneys and curry dishes. It is also an integral ingredient in Worcestershire sauce. It can be found in East Indian and Asian markets in various forms: jars of concentrated pulp, canned paste, whole pods dried into "bricks" or ground into powder.

Tamari:

(Say *tah-MAR-ee*.) Traditionally a by-product of miso, today "tamari" refers to a naturally brewed soy sauce that, unlike shoyu, contains no wheat. Tamari holds up well to cooking. It is somewhat thicker and richer than shoyu, which is better added after cooking, but otherwise the two products are much the same. Because there is some confusion between the terms "shoyu" and "tamari," people allergic to wheat should check the label to make sure the tamari they buy is wheat-free. Available in natural food stores, Asian markets and some supermarkets.

Tempeh:

(Say *TEM-pay*.) A high protein cultured food made from soybeans. It certainly is the most foreign-looking soy food around. Invented in Indonesia, tempeh is traditionally made by culturing cooked, cracked soybeans with the mold *Rhizopus oligosporus*. Some manufacturers offer tempeh made from grains rather than soybeans, or from a mixture of the two.

Tempeh has a firm, chewy texture and a mild, mushroom taste. It is commonly used to replace ground beef, chicken or fish in recipes. Truly a whole food, tempeh is a better nutritional bet than tofu. Unlike tofu, it must be cooked before eating. Refrigerated vacuum-packed tempeh will keep for about a week, or months frozen. Tempeh's culture shows white at first, then black; if you see many black spots, don't buy it. At home a few are okay, but the flavor will be stronger than all-white tempeh. Available in natural food stores, Asian markets, or it can be made at home.

Tofu:

Sometimes called "bean curd," tofu is a white, neutral tasting, easily digestible soy food. It is made by precipitating the solid proteins from soy milk with a mineral coagulant, a process similar to cheese making. Tofu is high in protein and contains no cholesterol. However, more than half of its calories come from fat, though the flavor and texture don't suggest it. Tofu can substitute for meat or cheese in many recipes, and readily picks up the flavors from other foods.

Tofu is available in several varieties. Soft and silken types are best in sauces, smoothies and dessert recipes; firmer styles are better for main dishes. Freezing and thawing tofu makes it firmer, drier and chewier – good for cubing into stir-fries and stews. One new innovation is flavored tofu, such as country herb or garlic. Tofu is highly perishable, so store it in water in its sealed package or a covered container until you're ready to use it. Fresh tofu should be rinsed daily and used within a week. Packaged tofu should be used before the date on the package. Many varieties of tofu are available in natural food stores, Oriental groceries, (where you'll even find it freeze-dried!) and many supermarkets. It can also be made at home.

Turbinado (or Demerara, or Raw) Sugar:

Actually a steam-cleaned version of sugar which retains a fraction of the dark, sticky molasses syrup produced in sugar refining. Any suggestion that this is an unrefined sugar is misleading. It is, however, not subject to the chemical whitening of common table sugar. Available in natural food stores.

Turmeric:

The fleshy root stalk of a brilliant tropical plant which belongs to the ginger family. It contains a bright yellow dye and is one of the principal ingredients in curries and other Far Eastern dishes. It is native to the Far East generally, and to parts of Africa and Australia. Even the color of the flower when grown in hot countries is a bright yellow, although that grown in China is a dull green. The root of the turmeric is irregularly shaped. The aroma is clean but the flavor is rather bitter and faintly resinous.

It has been used for centuries because of its color and its warmth of flavor. If used in moderation – i.e., a pinch – it can be used instead of saffron to give color to food. It is best bought in root form, but is also available powdered in the spice section of natural food stores and supermarkets.

Umeboshi:

(Say *OO-me-BO-she.*) A pink, slightly sour plum that has been pickled in salt. It is used *sparingly* as a condiment or salt substitute in salad dressings, sauces, rice or cooked vegetable dishes. It will keep for several years at room temperature. Store in an airtight glass jar to prevent dehydration. Available as whole plums, a thick paste or a salty, strong-flavored vinegar in Asian markets and natural food stores.

Wasabi:

A light green horseradish mustard. Available in paste and powdered form (mix powder with water to form a paste). Sold in natural food stores and Asian markets.

Wild Rice:

The nutty-tasting, dark brown seeds of a grass native to the Great Lakes region. Although not a grain, wild rice is used like one. It triples in volume when cooked. Because of its expense and strong taste, wild rice is usually used in combination with brown rice or other grains. It will keep indefinitely when stored in an airtight container in a cool, dry place.

Whole Wheat Flour:

This flour is made from winter or spring wheat which is high in gluten for bread making.

Whole Wheat Pastry Flour:

This flour is made from a completely different wheat berry than bread wheat. It is tan colored and low in gluten, therefore more appropriate for use in pastries.

WonderSlim:

The brand name of a fat and egg substitute used in baking, cooking and salad dressings. It is made from dried plums, water and unbleached lecithin. For baking, 1/4 cup of WonderSlim replaces 1/2 cup of butter, oil or margarine. Available in natural food stores and some supermarkets.

Zest:

The outermost rind of citrus fruits used as a seasoning and as a garnish.

GOOD SOURCES OF INFORMATION

Books

1. *The McDougall Program for a Healthy Heart* by Dr. John McDougall, Penguin Books, USA Inc., 375 Hudson Street, New York, NY 10014 (1996).

2. *The McDougall Program, 12 Days to Dynamic Health* by Dr. John McDougall, Penguin Books, USA Inc., 375 Hudson Street, New York, NY 10014 (1990).

3. *The McDougall Plan* by Dr. John McDougall, New Century Publishers Inc., 230 Old New Brunswick Road, Piscataway, N J 08854 (1983).

4. *The New McDougall Cookbook* by John McDougall, M.D. & Mary McDougall, Penguin Books, USA Inc., 375 Hudson Street, New York, NY 10014 (1990).

5. *McDougall's Medicine, A Challenging Second Opinion* by Dr. John McDougall, New Win Publishing, Inc., P.O. Box 5159, Clinton, NJ 08809 (1985).

6. *The McDougall Program for Maximum Weight Loss* by Dr. John McDougall, Penguin Books, USA Inc., 375 Hudson Street, New York, NY 10014 (1994).

7. *Save Yourself From Breast Cancer* by Dr. Robert M. Kradjian, NY Berkley Publishing Group (1994).

8. *Eat More, Weigh Less* by Dr. Dean Ornish, HarperCollins Publishers, Inc., 10 East 53rd Street, New York, NY 10022 (1993).

9. *Reversing Heart Disease* by Dr. Dean Ornish, Random House, Inc., NY (1990).

10. *Food for Life* by Dr. Neal Barnard, NY, Harmony Books, 201 East 50th Street, New York, NY 10022 (1993).

11. *The Power of Your Plate* by Dr. Neal Barnard, Book Publishing Company, P.O. Box 99, Summertown, TN 38483 (1990).

12. *Diet for a New America* by John Robbins, Stillpoint Publishing, Box 640, Walpole, NH 03608 (1987).
13. *May All Be Fed* by John Robbins, William Morrow and Company, Inc., 1350 Avenue of the Americas, New York, NY 10019 (1992).
14. *Long Life Now* by Lee Hitchcox, Celestial Arts, P.O. Box 7123, Berkeley, CA 94707 (1996).
15. *Healthy Heart Handbook* by Dr. Neal Pinckney, Healing Heart Foundation, 84-683 Upena Street, Makaha, HI 96792 (1994).
16. *Beyond Beef* by Jeremy Rifkin, Penguin Books, USA Inc., 375 Hudson Street, New York, NY 10014 (1992).
17. *The Surgeon General's Report on Nutrition and Health, Summary & Recommendations* by U.S. Department of Health and Human Services, Publication No. 88-50211 (1988).
18. *Food* by Susan Powter, Simon & Shuster, 1230 Avenue of the Americas, New York, NY 10020 (1995).
19. *A Quick Guide to Food Additives* by Robert Goodman, Silvercat Publications, San Diego, CA (1990).
20. *Health Unlimited* by Dr. Alan Immerman, Naturegrath Publishers, Inc., P.O. Box 1075, Happy Camp, CA 96039 (1989).

Videos

1. *The McDougall Program* by Dr. John McDougall.
2. *The McDougall Program for Maximum Weight Loss* by Dr. John McDougall.
3. *Diet for All Reasons* by Dr. Michael Klaper.
4. *Diet for a New America* by John Robbins.

Magazines & Publications

1. *Vegetarian Times*, P.O. Box 570, Oak Park, IL 60303; 800-435-9610
2. *Natural Health*, P.O. Box 7442, Red Oak, IA 51591.
3. *Health Science*, American Natural Hygiene Society, P.O. Box 30630, Tampa, FL 33630.
4. *Nutrition Advocate*, P.O. Box 4716, Ithaca, NY 14852.
5. *Bay Area Vegetarian*, Vegetarian Foundation, P.O. Box 9470, Stanford, CA 94309.
6. *The McDougall Newsletter*, P.O. Box 14039, Santa Rosa, CA 95402.
7. *Veggie Life*, 308 E. Hitt Street, P.O. Box 440, Mt. Morris, IL 61054.

Resources for Unusual Products

1. *Tic Gums, Inc.*, 4609 Richlynn Drive, Belcamp, MD 21017, 800 221-3953 (supplier to natural food stores).
2. *Ener-G Foods, Inc.*, P.O. Box 84487, Seattle, WA 98124, 800-331-5222 (supplier of Egg Replacer plus other products; supplier to natural food stores).
3. *King Arthur Flour*, P.O. Box 876, Norwich, VT 05055, 800-827-6836 (catalog).
4. *Trinity Herbs*, P.O. Box 199, Bodega, CA 94922, 707-874-3418 (catalog).

Index

Agar-Agar, 240
Aioli, roasted red pepper, 33
Alfredo sauce, 40
Amazake, 240
Apples
    baked yams and, 154-155
    pie, 218-219
    preparation, 224
Apricot
    ginger pie, 200
    teriyaki rice salad, 78
Aram rolls, 24
    roasted red pepper aioli filling, 33
    spicy red safrito filling, 35
Arrowroot, 240
Arroz Mexicana, 100
Artichoke, salad, 79
Asparagus
    with curry sauce, 104
    salad, 80
    soup, 122

Baba ghanouj
    acorn squash, 22
    eggplant, 25

Baking, methods, 230
Balsamic vinegar, 240-241
Bananas
    baked, 201
    raisin muffins, 10
    milk, 9
Barley
    mushroom soup, 137
    spring loaf/burger, 188-189
Basmati rice, 241
BBQ sauce, 41
Beans
    adzuki pâté, 23
    anasaki, 124-125
    black, 44, 124-127, 153
    fagioli, 244
    fiesta chili, 166-167

and "franks," 177
green, 111
kidney, 124-125, 166-167, 177
lima, 147
minestrone soup, 133
mung bean potato casserole, 175
navy, 96, 149
oven baked, 177
pinto, 124-125
pinto bean pâté, 26
preparation, 224
soup du jour, 124-125
Tuscan bean salad, 96
Tuscan soup, 146-147
white, 146
white bean Florentine soup, 149
See also Garbanzo
"Beef," broth powder, 229
Beets
    cherry borscht, 123
    in citrus dressing, 102
    salad, 81
    winter salad, 97
Biscuit
    basic dough, 11
    sweet, 220
Blueberry
    muffins, 14
    topping, 206
Boiling, methods, 230
Bolognese sauce, 43
Bragg Liquid Aminos, 241
Breads
    basic yeast dough, 12-13
    fruited roll ups, 19
    pizza with roasted peppers and veggies, 30
    See also Quick breads
Breakfast
    menu planning, 8
    muffins, 14
Broccoli
    and cauliflower melange, 103
    with curry sauce, 104